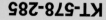

Physical Characteristics of the Pharaoh Hound

(from the American Kennel Club breed standard)

Size: Height—Dogs 23 inches–25 inches. Bitches 21 inches–24 inches. All over balance must be maintained.

Coat: Short and glossy, ranging from fine and close to slightly harsh with no feathering.

Tail: Medium set—fairly thick at the base and tapering whip-like, reaching below the point of hock in repose. Well carried and curved when in action. The tail should not be tucked between the legs.

Hindquarters: Strong and muscular. Limbs parallel. Moderate sweep of stifle. Well developed second thigh. Dewclaws may be removed. Feet as in front.

Pharaoh Hound

◇

By Juliette Cunliffe

Contents

KENNEL CLUB BOOKS: **PHARAOH HOUND**
ISBN: 1-59378-342-6

Copyright © 2004
Kennel Club Books, Inc., 308 Main Street, Allenhurst, NJ 07711 USA
Cover Design Patented: US 6,435,559 B2 • Printed in South Korea

Photographs by Isabelle Français and Carol Ann Johnson
with additional photographs by
Norvia Behling, T.J. Calhoun, Carolina Biological Supply, Doskocil, James Hayden-Yoav, James R. Hayden, RBP, Bill Jonas, Dwight R. Kuhn, Dr. Dennis Kunkel, Mikki Pet Products, Phototake, Jean Claude Revy and Dr. Andrew Spielman, Alice van Kempen and Doreen M. Wright.

Illustrations by Patricia Peters.

The publisher would like to thank the owners of all of the dogs featured in this book, including Jan Butterworth, Lori Evans, Gregory & Lisa Mitrosky, Jill & David Morris, Marilyn M. Smith.

One of the ancient breeds of dogdom, the Pharaoh Hound is an intriguing sighthound whose history spans thousands of years.

HISTORY OF THE

PHARAOH HOUND

THE PHARAOH HOUND IN ANCIENT HISTORY

The Pharaoh Hound ranks among the oldest of domestic dogs recorded in history, indeed some say it is the very oldest. This red hound was a great favorite of Egyptian nobles and was known 3,000 years or so before Christ, for there are many murals on tombstones and on papyrus, depicting a remarkably similar middle-sized sighthound with erect ears.

Anubis, who in Egyptian mythology was considered the inventor of embalming, as well as being guardian of tombs and judge of the dead, is often said to resemble today's Pharaoh Hound. However, it must be said that there is still controversy among Egyptologists as to whether Anubis was a dog or a jackal.

Indeed the history of this captivating breed is a little controversial, and it is not always easy to distinguish between fact and fiction. While the majority of enthusiasts clearly believe that the Pharaoh Hound was one of the hounds of Egypt, there are others who claim that, under the name of Kelb Tal-Fenek, this breed really has its roots in Malta. Supporters of this theory believe that in Egypt

Anubis, ancient Egyptian god of death, has been represented by a dog-like figure with erect ears and a pointed snout. This painted wooden statue is dated about 300 BC.

itself, this dog was considered to be of Maltese origin. Whatever one chooses to believe about this breed's early origin, there is no disputing the fact that these hounds have been preserved in Malta for many a long year. They have been bred for hunting rabbit, as well as for guarding the homesteads, many standing picturesquely on look-out from the flat rooftops.

Over time, dedicated researchers have concluded that the Pharaoh Hound is in fact a mixture of *Canis doerdelini*, *Canis lupaster* and pariahs. From the first, the breed obtained its elegant silhouette; from the second, its beautiful limbs; from the last, its erect ears and gentle nature.

Going back to dogs of this type in ancient Egypt, there is evidence that such dogs were used primarily to hunt hare, gazelle, antelope and ibex (a type of wild goat). It is also fascinating to note that in Egypt, not only humans but also dogs were mummified, and mummies of dogs measuring 22 inches (56 cm) at the shoulder have been discovered. Such mummification ensured that they could enter the afterlife. When Tutankhamen's burial chamber was opened, among the treasures was a life-sized dog resembling a Pharaoh Hound, and inside a mummified dog.

Pliny the Elder (23–79), the Roman writer and encyclopedist who was the foremost authority on science in ancient Egypt, wrote

The burial chamber of Pashedu, dated about 1200 BC, is guarded by two Anubis dogs.

Front (left) and back (right) sides of a slate carved between 6000 and 5000 BC, depicting ancient dogs hunting gazelle.

Left to right: One of the dogs depicted on the tomb of Antefa II; an ancient Egyptian pet dog; "Akbaru," the Khufu dog.

on quadrupeds. He mentioned the red dog, saying that because its hearing was so good, it was tethered along the Nile so that it could watch out for intruders and give warning of their approach. These red dogs were also sacrificed to the gods.

THE PHARAOH HOUND IN MALTA

The Phoenicians were seafarers who arrived in Malta in pre-Christian times. When they settled on the islands of Malta and Gozo, they took with them their hounds. In Malta, the Pharaoh Hound is therefore believed to have existed for over 2,000 years. It was here that the breed developed, unaffected by outside influence, with the result that this hound breeds very true to type.

However, the earliest written reference to the breed in Malta was in 1647, when Commendatore Fra. G. Fran Abela wrote of dogs called "Cernechi," which were "esteemed for the hunting of rabbits." They were "in demand primarily for stony, mountainous and steep locations." We should thus also consider that there was a long gap between this date and the decline of the Pharaonic Empire.

Whether or not one accepts that these Maltese islands were the original home of the breed, there is no doubt that the dogs have been preserved here by the inhabitants who know them as Kelb Tal-Fenek. However, for simplicity's sake, I hope the Maltese will forgive the author for using the name Pharaoh Hound, for this is the name by which the breed is known more generally in most countries throughout the world.

A theory upheld by exponents of the breed in Malta is that the Pharaoh Hound might well be a descendant of the ancient type of prick-eared hound that is found in many different cultures around the Mediterranean Sea. As one finds with many closely associated breeds in various groups, it is understandable that, over time, specific breeds developed in their own countries. In Portugal, we find the Podengo Português; in the Balearic Islands, the Podenco Ibicenco or Ibizan Hound; in the Canary Islands, the Podenco Canario; and in Sicily, the Cirneco dell' Etna. In Malta, the Pharaoh Hound has undoubtedly become a

A HUNTING HOUND

In Malta, the Pharaoh Hound, or Kelb Tal-Fenek, as he is known there, hunts not only rabbit but also quail and woodcock. When hunting birds, the dog searches out, then flushes the birds, so that they can be shot down by the hunter. Just a few hunters also train their Pharaohs to retrieve the birds when shot, as well as to retrieve the rabbits they have killed.

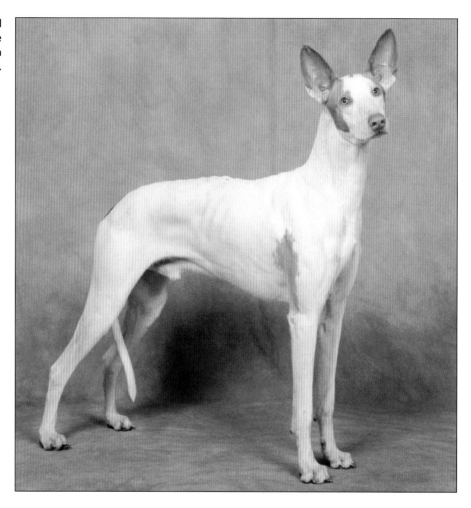

native of that country and until a
few decades ago they were not
known outside Malta. However,
since then, they have spread to
many countries of the world.

The Pharaoh Hound, known
there of course as the Kelb Tal-
Fenek, is held in such high
esteem in Malta that, in 1974, it
was declared the country's
National Dog. In 1977, a Maltese
Lira coin was minted, depicting
this distinctive breed of dog on its
reverse.

USE AS A RABBIT DOG

In earlier years, it was necessary
for people in Malta to hunt rabbit
for food, for life could be hard.
Today, though, rabbit hunting is

Head study of a
rough-coated
Ibizan Hound.

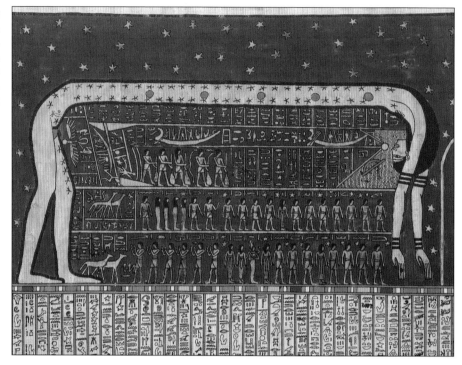

considered more of a sport and a means of keeping a tradition alive. The breed in Malta is today used for hunting, primarily by farmers who keep several dogs, utilizing their cooperative abilities. Often they work with a dog and bitch, which they call a "couple," and selection of dogs is based on hunting ability. In this way, the efficiency of the breed has been preserved.

Although rabbits in Malta are exceedingly nimble, jumping easily from one stone to the next over difficult, rocky terrain, they tend not to dig burrows. Rather, they take refuge under rocks and in the walls of rubble. Near the coast, they hide inside cracks and crevices. Dogs that have been bred to work in this rugged landscape need to be tough and well-built, as is the Pharaoh Hound.

These hounds have a remark-ably good sense of smell for a sighthound. They work away from the wind so that they can get the smell of the rabbit early, while the rabbit does not notice the approach of the dogs. It is also interesting to note that the dogs are keen to roll in rabbit droppings, a further way of concealing their approach as their scent is thus disguised. Endurance is high and these hounds can work all night if necessary. If worked during daylight hours, the dog stands considerably less chance of surprising a rabbit, for the dog announces his location of the prey by barking and enthusiastic scratching.

When the dog brings the hunter's attention to a hidden rabbit, the hunter employs a ferret, carried in a basket and wearing a little bell. As the ferret moves along in inaccessible places, the dog can follow the sound of the ferret until the rabbit bolts. For readers who are wondering about the relationship between dog and ferret, in Malta they both grow up together, so the Pharaoh Hounds do not consider the ferrets as prey, and, in any case, the dogs respect their sharp teeth!

Of course there are occasions on which a dog loses sight of its prey, in which case the Pharaoh Hound will search the area in ever-widening circles until located again. On difficult ground, the dog will sometimes jump high to become oriented. At the kill, the Pharaoh Hound grips the rabbit by biting into its neck or back, then shaking it until dead.

THE PHARAOH HOUND ARRIVES IN BRITAIN

Mrs. Shoppe of Dulverton in Somerset, UK, is responsible for registering the first Pharaoh Hound imported to Europe. She knew that other Pharaoh Hounds had been brought into the country by servicemen but she found no trace of these when she endeavored to put her own dog to stud.

Her Pharaoh did, however, have the distinction of being portrayed in *Hutchinson's Encyclopaedia*, published in the early 1930s. There were two photographs, under the name Kelb Tal-Fenek, with the comment that this breed was an excellent friend to its owners and made a good watchdog. Of interest is that, each season, Mrs. Shoppe's Pharaoh hunted with the Quantock Stag Hounds.

As you may have anticipated, the breed did not thrive in Britain. Fortunately, though, in the 1960s, Major General Adam Block, commanding in the Mediterranean, purchased and imported

WHAT'S IN A NAME?
The original breed name applied for in Britain was Kelb Tal-Fenek, the literal translation of which is "rabbit dog," though a more precise translation is actually "rabbit-hunting dog" or "rabbit hound." This application was refused on the grounds that it was "unacceptable," but some people still rightly wonder why this was so. After all, we do have Otterhounds, Foxhounds and even Dachshunds, which when, translated from German, means "badger dog."

Bahri of Twinley in 1962, this with his wife, Pauline. Further imports followed: Twinley Valletta, Chu-Cha and Luki, Pupa and Sibuna Ziff. Some of these were owned in partnership with Mr. and Mrs. Liddell Grainer and Mrs. Anne Dewey, who was to become the first secretary of the breed club.

Until this time the breed was still known as the Kelb Tal-Fenek, which, in translation meant "rabbit dog." The English Kennel Club, however, refused to

SIGHT, SCENT AND SOUND HOUND

Although classified as a sighthound, the Pharaoh Hound actually uses both sight and smell when hunting his prey. The breed also has an acute sense of hearing.

In America and Britain, the Pharaoh Hound is exhibited in the Hound Group, and under the FCI it falls into Group Five, which is for "Spitz and Primitive types."

Mrs. Shoppe's Kelb Tal-Fenek, the first of this breed in Britain.

register the breed, stating that the name was totally unacceptable because it translated merely to "rabbit dog." As a result, Pauline Block and Anne Dewey contacted the Fédération Cynologique Internationale (FCI), inquiring what name they used for this breed. The reply, received in November 1965, said that "the race bred in Malta is recognized by the FCI as the Pharaoh Hound." So it was that the name Pharaoh Hound came into use in Britain, although the Maltese name Kelb Tal-Fenek appeared in brackets alongside the name.

In 1972, Lionel Hamilton-Renwick imported hounds from Gozo, and in 1973 and 1974 there were further importations. The English Kennel Club granted the breed full recognition in 1974, giving permission for Challenge

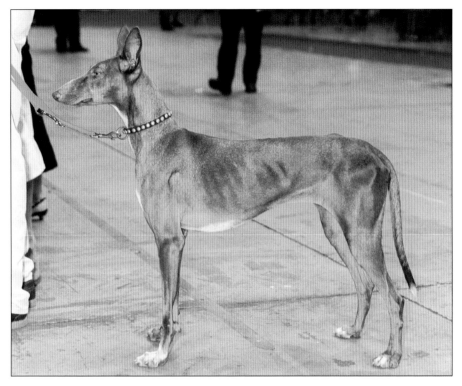

The Podenco Canario is a related breed that is similar in looks to the Pharaoh Hound.

Certificates to be awarded, something that was to happen in 1975. The breed's first champion, Kilcroney Rekhmire Merymut, a male, was bred by Mrs. G. Le Strange-West and co-owned by the highly successful partnership of Miss Monica Still, Dr. Christine Singer and Dr. Jeanne Druce. These three ladies, founders of the Merymut Kennels, had visited Egypt, where they were fascinated by the prick-eared hounds they had seen on tombs. In a Harley Street dental office, they later came across an article about the breed, written by Lionel Hamilton-Renwick, and so began the Merymut dynasty.

Eng. Ch. Kilcroney Rekhmire Merymut, a natural extrovert who loved the sound of applause, did much to promote the breed before championship status was granted. The first bitch to gain her championship title in the UK was the second champion in the breed, Tarnach Twinley Xamxi, bred by Pauline Block and owned by Liz Waugh. Eng. Ch. Talkaccatur Bardaxxa is also worthy of note, for this was the first of the Maltese imports to gain a title in Britain.

THE PHARAOH HOUND IN THE US

The Pharaoh Hound first arrived in the US in 1967, and the first litter was whelped in 1970, when the breed's parent club, the Pharaoh Hound Club of America, was founded. The breed was accepted into the American Kennel Club's Miscellaneous Class in 1973, and recognized for registration in the AKC's Stud Book in 1983. On January 1, 1984, it was entered into the Hound Group, becoming eligible for full championship status in America. The breed ranks in the lower quarter in registration statistics with about 100 puppies registered annually.

In the US, the Pharaoh Hound takes part in lure-coursing field trials, which are open to all breeds of sighthound and in which they gain titles by carrying out the work for which they were originally bred. In such trials, the hounds chase a white plastic bag, representing a rabbit, and no live game is used. They also take part in open field coursing, though this is primarily available only on the West Coast. Obedience trials are also popular competitive events, but because Pharaohs can be somewhat stubborn, they rarely accomplish competitive obedience titles.

Pharaoh Hounds at an outdoor dog show. This intriguing breed attracts much interest and attention in the show ring.

Pharaoh owners are very proud of their dogs and fascinated by the breed's history and personality. Good specimens can be found world-wide.

CHARACTERISTICS OF THE
PHARAOH HOUND

The Pharaoh Hound is a unique breed, both in appearance and in temperament, and of course its history is thoroughly fascinating. An extremely intelligent dog, the Pharaoh Hound is playful and loving, and yet also dignified and, as some people put it, "self-contained."

The Pharaoh Hound is absolutely not a suitable breed for everyone; it can be very demanding and has a mind of its own. Owners should therefore think long and hard before making the decision to own one, always keeping uppermost in their minds that this is a breed that was selectively bred for hunting, and, even after such a long period of time, the hunting instinct is still strong.

PERSONALITY

The personality of the Pharaoh Hound is quite different from that of most other breeds. Pharaohs are devoted to their owners and enjoy being with them, but they are unlikely to pester their owners for visible affection. Although they like to be loved, they will decide when they want this attention. This is a sociable breed, one that enjoys companionship, be it of humans or other dogs. There is no

DOGS, DOGS, GOOD FOR YOUR HEART!

People usually purchase dogs for companionship, but studies show that dogs can help to improve their owners' health and level of activity, as well as lower a human's risk of coronary heart disease. Without even realizing it, when a person puts time into exercising, grooming and feeding a dog, he also puts more time into his own personal health care. Dog owners establish more routine schedules for their dogs to follow, which can have positive effects on their own health. Dogs also teach us patience, offer unconditional love and provide the joy of having a furry friend to pet!

doubt that, if given the opportunity, a Pharaoh Hound will enjoy the comfort of an easy chair and have absolutely no objection to sleeping on (or under) the blankets at night. When taking on a Pharaoh, it is therefore important to start as you mean to go on!

With strangers, the breed can be rather reserved, and this tends to apply rather more to the females than to the males. Pharaohs like to take their time to get to know guests, but once they have accepted them, those guests can expect a warm welcome on future visits. This breed is highly alert, making it a good watchdog, likely to bark loudly at the approach of a stranger or visitor to the house.

By nature, the Pharaoh Hound is an entertainer, one that seems to thoroughly enjoy making his owners laugh at his antics. Everything this hound does is looked upon by him as something that can be a potential game, and so it should come as no surprise that the Pharaoh Hound rarely adapts easily to traditional training. But success can be achieved, provided that an owner is consistent, fair and gentle.

A Pharaoh Hound can be quite stubborn when the fancy takes him. Although Pharaohs understand a lot of what is said to them, they usually don't seem to understand until the second time

THE ALLURE OF LURE COURSING

Pharaoh Hounds greatly enjoy lure coursing, giving the dog an opportunity to experience the joy of the chase, without taking live prey. In some countries, such as Denmark, it is forbidden to hunt live game, so lure coursing is a means of satisfying the dogs' natural desire to run and to chase.

it is said! Actually, they learn very quickly, but they learn the bad things too, not only the good. Not a bad thing, I suppose, but one of my favorite stories about the breed I love most is of the Pharaoh Hound who jumps up to pick his own apples off a tree in his owner's garden. It is said that

Pharaohs don't wait for anything to happen by itself, but instead make an active contribution to life around them.

They love to play and, in fact, often respond best when they know that what they do will make their owners laugh. However, they should not be played with roughly, and it should always be borne in mind that they hate to feel trapped or cornered. Curious dogs, they have a tendency to steal things, and many owners say it is sensible to "Pharaoh-proof" the house, so as to avoid finding little things missing. It is not unknown for a Pharaoh to steal the towel when his owner is in the bathtub or shower, whisking it away through the house, only to hide it in some inaccessible place! When their owners are not at home, most Pharaohs are kept in a room where they can do no harm, in a kennel run or in a large crate.

Pharaoh Hounds are known for their wizardry in the art of escape, so tall, sturdy fencing and watchful eyes are necessary on the part of Pharaoh Hound owners.

A HAPPY COMPANION

Pharaoh Hounds are affectionate to family members and most enjoy participating in family life if given the opportunity. They are naturally clean dogs with no doggy odor. Dogs whose owners spend too little time with them have a way of looking miserably unhappy and bored.

Pharaoh Hounds are sensitive dogs and should never be punished physically. Raising your voice in reprimand is quite enough. Indeed, Pharaohs have the rather charming habit of blushing when they are excited, their nose and the insides of their ears turning to a deep mauve. This is a dog that can also "smile" when he is happy; this he does by wrinkling the corner of his lips up over his teeth.

ESCAPE AND CHASE

The Pharaoh Hounds have especially clever feet, and most seem capable of opening any door they choose. They retain the chasing instinct of their ancestors, so should only be allowed off-lead in places where you can be absolutely certain they can come to no harm. Always remember that they are capable of sprinting at full speed for great distances.

PHARAOHS WITH CHILDREN AND OTHER PETS

Provided introductions are made under careful supervision while the dog is still young, Pharaoh Hounds can get along very well with children and with other pets. In Malta, when these dogs are kept on farms, it is frequently the children of the family who are responsible for feeding and grooming them. It is often said that Pharaoh Hounds see children as potential playmates. It goes without saying that owners must, however, teach dogs and children to respect each other from the very first introduction, and young children with dogs should always be kept under close supervision.

It should also be considered that, although Pharaoh Hounds can get along well with other pets in the family if introduced carefully from the outset, if not restrained, they will almost certainly chase any neighborhood cats, as well as rabbits and the furry like!

PHYSICAL CHARACTERISTICS

This is a breed that is noted for its clean-cut lines and its graceful yet powerful appearance. The body is lithe, with an almost straight topline, and the deep brisket extends down to the point of elbow. It is worthy of note that this is dissimilar to that of the Ibizan Hound, in which there can be a distance of 2.5–3 inches

JUMPING PHARAOHS!
The Pharaoh Hound is particularly nimble, with extraordinary jumping power. When hunting, he is highly attentive and is very much aware of the type of terrain on which he is working, giving care to where he treads. He is also clearly aware that his prey is likely to alter direction or to bolt into shelter, and this can be noticed in his style of running.

between the bottom of the rib cage and the elbow.

Shoulders are strong, long and well-laid back, forelegs straight and parallel, with strong pasterns. The hindquarters are strong and muscular, with a moderate bend of stifle and a well-developed second thigh. Viewed from behind, the limbs should be parallel. Feet are strong, firm and well knuckled, with the paws well padded.

The movement of the Pharaoh Hound is free and flowing, covering the ground without apparent effort. The head is held high, and legs and feet should move in line with the body.

HEAD AND EARS
With its long skull and well-chiseled contours, the head of the Pharaoh Hound represents a blunt wedge when viewed both in profile and from above, with only a slight stop between skull and muzzle. The amber color of the oval, moderately deep-set eyes blends with the coat, giving a keen, intelligent expression. The nose is flesh-colored, again blending with the coat.

The fine, large ears of the Pharaoh Hound are very special. They are broad at the base and carried erect when alert, but are very mobile indeed. Although this is a sighthound, it understandably has spectacularly good hearing, too. When a Pharaoh is fully alert, with the ears erect, his forehead wrinkles, creating the appearance of intense concentration.

TAIL
The tail is set on at medium height and is fairly thick at the base, tapering whip-like to the end, where a white tip is highly

Small pets may incite the Pharaoh Hound's chase instinct; many do best with larger pets, like other dogs, as housemates. This Pharaoh and his German Shepherd friend take a break to cool off.

desirable. When the dog is in motion, the tail is carried high and curved. At other times, it is carried in repose, but should not be tucked between the legs.

SIZE

This is a fairly large breed, with dogs standing between 22–25 inches, and bitches between 21–24 inches at the withers.

COAT

The Pharaoh Hound has a short glossy coat, which ranges from fine and close to slightly harsh. There is no feathering on the Pharaoh Hound's coat.

Until the age of about three years, a Pharaoh Hound will have two full sheddings each year, following which there is a continuous light shedding. During the heavy shedding in the dog's youth, the coat will deepen in color after each shedding, usually commencing on the skull, then in a line along the back and eventually down the sides.

COLOR

The color of the Pharaoh Hound is very striking. It is tan or rich tan, and although some white markings are allowed, these must be in keeping with the details set down in the breed standard. Flecking in the coat, or white markings other than those specified, are undesirable.

LURE-COURSING CONSIDERATIONS

Pharaoh Hounds are good at lure coursing and follow the lure for the simple joy of giving chase. Watching a Pharaoh fly around a course, you can become immediately aware of the breed's tremendous athleticism. Lure coursing is a fun and exciting way to simulate a real hunt, though this does not give the hound the opportunity to turn and manipulate, as would be the case when chasing live prey.

If participating in lure coursing, it is sensible to allow Pharaoh Hounds to warm up and stretch out before they have an opportunity to sprint at full speed. Afterwards, if they are walked a while, they have a chance to cool down, preventing stiffness. They should be encouraged to drink lots of water for re-hydration and should be allowed ample opportunity to urinate to shed lactic acid.

TEETH

This breed has powerful jaws and strong teeth, with a scissors bite, the upper teeth closely overlapping the lower ones and set square to the jaws.

HEALTH CONSIDERATIONS

The Pharaoh Hound is generally a very healthy breed and appears to be free of many of the genetic problems that have plagued other breeds, such as hip dysplasia and eye disorders. However, to be forewarned is to be forearmed, so the following section of this chapter pinpoints a few problems in the breed about which an owner should be aware, so that any problems encountered can be dealt with as early as possible.

Undescended Testicles

Unilateral cryptorchidism is undoubtedly a genetic problem within this breed, and although dogs that are thus affected can produce sperm, they should never be used at stud. This condition indicates the retention of one testicle, due in this case usually to a shortening of the cord, thus not allowing the testicle to drop. Unilateral cryptorchidism is often referred to erroneously as monorchidism, but in fact this is different; the latter is a condition in which only one testicle is present. Veterinary advice should be sought regarding whether or not removal of the undescended testicle is advisable.

Patellar Luxation

Some Pharaoh Hounds have been known to suffer from patella luxation, a substandard formation of the knee joint that affects a number of breeds, though more often the smaller ones. Depending on where you live, this condition may still be a problem, though in the US and UK it has been largely eradicated over the last ten years.

In mild cases, there may be no evident signs of the problem, but, if more severe, patellar luxation can be both painful and disabling, one of the signs being that a leg is lifted intermittently. The hind legs can become bowed and the gait altered, and, in the long term, arthritis can develop. Occasionally surgery is necessary and any dog seriously affected should certainly not be bred from.

Careful breeders have their stock tested for patellar luxation, and some also have the test for hip dysplasia performed at the

PREVENTING ESCAPISM

Houdini had nothing on the Pharaoh Hound for escape artistry! This is a lithe and athletic breed; many of them seem to have an uncanny way of opening doors. Some owners feel it prudent to crate-train Pharaohs for the dogs' own safety. It is absolutely essential that they have a secure environment in which to live, ideally with plenty of area with safe boundary fencing for a free run.

same time. Hip dysplasia, though, appears not to be a problem in the Pharaoh Hound.

REACTIONS TO INJECTIONS AND INSECTICIDES

Like other sighthounds, Pharaohs can suffer from reactions to modern-day injections. The reason for this seems to be that they lack the protective layer of fat under the skin, something that the majority of breeds have. This is something that should be discussed with your vet when injections are needed, and is especially important in the case of anesthetics. Some Pharaoh Hounds can also display sensitivity to insecticides, so this should be taken into account when selecting products for the control of parasites.

LATE FIRST SEASON

It is not unusual for a Pharaoh Hound to have her first season at a very late age, sometimes later than two years old. However, after the first heat cycle, her seasons will usually settle down into a regular cycle. Should she not have had a season at all by the age of three years, veterinary advice should be sought.

SOFT EARS

Although not concerning the health of the hound, a problem within the breed is "soft ears." This means that the ears do not

SENSITIVE AND BLUSHING

Pharaoh Hounds can both smile and blush, and many consider them among the most sensitive and expressive canines. They are not, however, a suitable breed for everyone, and potential owners who have lots of time and love for a new dog should do their homework thoroughly before deciding that the Pharaoh Hound is really the breed for them.

ONE BRIGHT HOUND

Pharaoh Hounds can be somewhat stubborn and seem to enjoy outsmarting their owners. They like to feel they are taking an active part in the decision-making and can refuse to do anything they deem unnecessary. However, with patience and a good sense of humor, an owner can teach his Pharaoh most things, and a lesson once learned is never forgotten.

stand erect as they should. Sometimes they stick up just slightly, resembling the ears of some terriers, but sometimes never at all. Pharaoh Hounds with correct ears should have them up by the age of six months.

MISSING PRE-MOLARS

A few Pharaoh Hounds have missing pre-molar teeth. Again this is not really a health issue, but the matter should be addressed in order that this is not allowed to become prevalent.

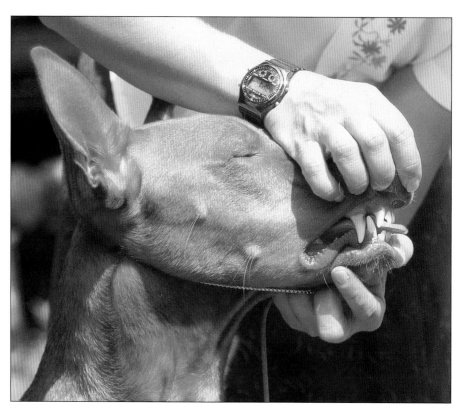

The correct bite for the Pharaoh Hound is strong teeth set in a scissors bite.

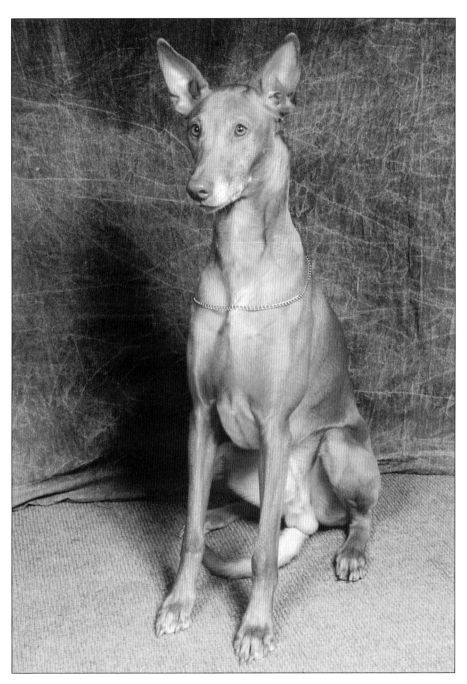

The breed standard calls for erect ears. Correct ear set and carriage contribute to the Pharaoh Hound's alert expression and are an important feature of the breed.

BREED STANDARD FOR THE

PHARAOH HOUND

INTRODUCTION TO THE BREED STANDARD

Written by the breed's parent club, the Pharaoh Hound Club of America, the breed standard, essentially a description of the ideal representative of the breed, is approved by the American Kennel Club (AKC). The way standards are formulated and approved, and the exact wording of the standard, vary from country to country, though are basically describing the same dog. There is some variation in word choice and emphasis, completeness and naming of faults/disqualifications. Of course, breed standards can be changed occasionally, and such changes come about with guidance from experienced people within the breed clubs.

All breed standards are designed effectively to paint a picture in words, though each reader will almost certainly have a slightly different way of interpreting these words. After all, when all is said and done, were everyone to interpret a breed's standard in exactly the same way, there would only be one consistent winner within the breed at any given time!

That said, certain things are made eminently clear in the standard. We know, for example, that the Pharaoh Hound's length of body from breast to haunch bone (hip) should be slightly longer than the height at withers. This is a straightforward statement of fact, so the reader can tell immediately that if the body is not a little longer than the dog is tall, the animal would not be suitably balanced for this breed. We also read that the eye is amber in color, and that the nose is flesh-colored, so a dog with a black nose and very dark eyes would be highly untypical.

In any event, to fully comprehend the intricacies of a breed, reading words alone is never enough. In addition, it is essential for devotees to watch Pharaoh Hounds being judged at shows and, if possible, to attend seminars at which the breed is discussed. This enables owners to absorb as much as possible about this highly individual breed. Hands-on experience, providing an opportunity to assess the structure of dogs, is always valuable, especially for those who hope ultimately to judge the breed.

The breed standard is the official description of the ideal Pharaoh Hound. The closer the dog adheres to the standard, the better are his chances of success in the show ring. This prize-winner is a stunning example of the breed.

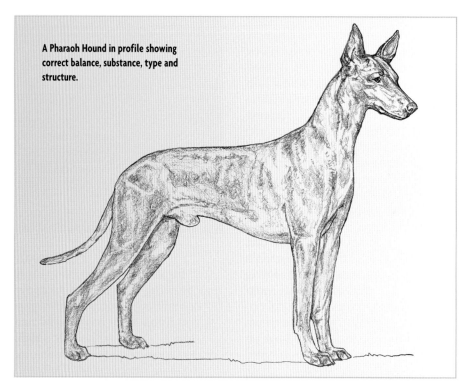

A Pharaoh Hound in profile showing correct balance, substance, type and structure.

However familiar you are with the breed, it is worth refreshing your memory by re-reading the standard, for it is sometimes all too easy to overlook, or perhaps conveniently forget, certain features. A breed standard undoubtedly helps breeders to produce stock that comes as close as possible to the recognized standard, and helps judges to know exactly what they are looking for. This enables judges to make carefully considered decisions when selecting the most typical Pharaoh Hound present to head the line of winners.

THE AMERICAN KENNEL CLUB STANDARD FOR THE PHARAOH HOUND

General Appearance: General Appearance is one of grace, power and speed. The Pharaoh Hound is medium sized, of noble bearing with hard clean-cut lines— graceful, well balanced, very fast with free easy movement and alert expression.

The following description is that of the ideal Pharaoh Hound. Any deviation from the below described dog must be penalized to the extent of the deviation.

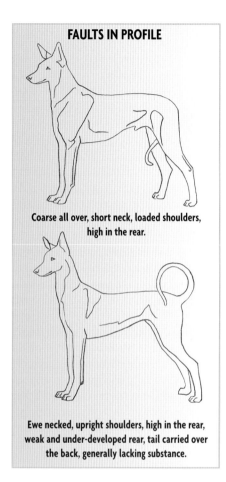

FAULTS IN PROFILE

Coarse all over, short neck, loaded shoulders, high in the rear.

Ewe necked, upright shoulders, high in the rear, weak and under-developed rear, tail carried over the back, generally lacking substance.

with keen intelligent expression. Ears medium high set, carried erect when alert, but very mobile, broad at the base, fine and large. Skull long, lean and chiseled. Only slight stop. Foreface slightly longer than the skull. Top of the skull parallel with the foreface representing a blunt wedge. Nose flesh colored, blending with the coat. No other color. Powerful jaws with strong teeth. Scissors bite.

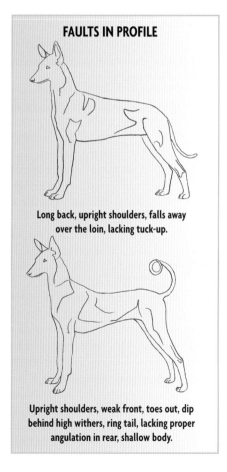

FAULTS IN PROFILE

Long back, upright shoulders, falls away over the loin, lacking tuck-up.

Upright shoulders, weak front, toes out, dip behind high withers, ring tail, lacking proper angulation in rear, shallow body.

Size, Proportion, Substance:
Height—Dogs 23 inches–25 inches. Bitches 21 inches–24 inches. All over balance must be maintained. Length of body from breast to haunch bone slightly longer than height of withers to ground. Lithe.

Head: Alert expression. Eyes amber colored, blending with coat; oval, moderately deep set

Head study of correct type and proportion.

Some Pharaoh Hounds are solid tan, while others have white markings. Certain white markings are acceptable as detailed in the standard.

Neck, Topline, Body: Neck long, lean and muscular with a slight arch to carry the head on high. Clean throat line. Almost straight topline. Slight slope from croup to root of tail. Body lithe. Deep brisket almost down to point of elbow. Ribs well sprung. Moderate tuck-up. Tail medium set—fairly thick at the base and tapering whip-like, reaching below the point of hock in repose. Well carried and curved when in action. The tail should not be tucked between the legs. A screw tail is a fault.

Forequarters: Shoulders long and sloping and well laid back. Strong without being loaded. Elbows well tucked in. Forelegs straight and parallel. Pasterns strong. Dewclaws may be removed. Feet neither cat nor hare but strong, well knuckled and firm, turning neither in nor out. Paws well padded.

Hindquarters: Strong and muscular. Limbs parallel. Moderate sweep of stifle. Well developed second thigh. Dewclaws may be removed. Feet as in front.

Coat: Short and glossy, ranging from fine and close to slightly harsh with no feathering. Accident blemishes should not be considered as faults.

Color: Ranging from tan/rich, tan/chestnut with white markings allowed as follows: White tip on tail strongly desired. White on chest (called "the Star"). White on toes and slim white snip on center-line of face permissible. Flecking or other white undesirable, except for any solid white spot on the

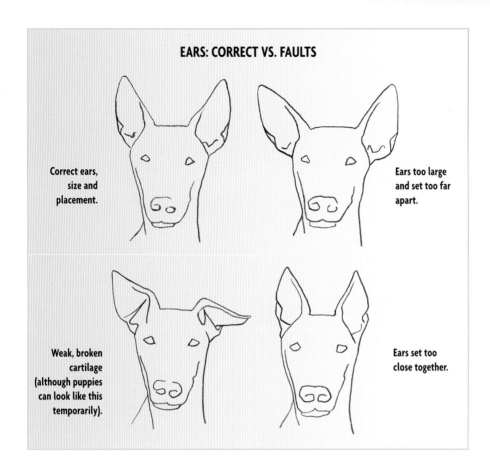

EARS: CORRECT VS. FAULTS

Correct ears, size and placement.

Ears too large and set too far apart.

Weak, broken cartilage (although puppies can look like this temporarily).

Ears set too close together.

back of neck, shoulder, or any part of the back or sides of the dog, which is a disqualification.

Gait: Free and flowing; the head should be held fairly high and the dog should cover the ground well without any apparent effort. The legs and feet should move in line with the body; any tendency to throw the feet sideways, or a high stepping "hackney" action is a definite fault.

Temperament: Intelligent, friendly, affectionate and playful. Alert and active. Very fast with a marked keenness for hunting, both by sight and scent.

Disqualification: Any solid white spot on the back of neck, shoulder, or any part of the back or sides of the dog.

Approved May 10, 1983
Effective April 3, 1989

PHARAOH HOUND

HOW TO SELECT A PUPPY

Before reaching the decision that you will definitely look for a Pharaoh Hound puppy, it is essential that you are fully clear in your mind that this is absolutely the most suitable breed, both for you and for your family. There is no disputing the fact that this is a very special breed, and all the pros and cons must be carefully weighed against each other before reaching the important decision that a Pharaoh Hound is going to enter your life.

When you have made that decision, you must also ask

YOUR SCHEDULE . . .
If you lead an erratic, unpredictable life, with daily or weekly changes in your work requirements, consider the problems of owning a puppy. The new puppy has to be fed regularly, socialized (loved, petted, handled, introduced to other people) and, most importantly, allowed to go outdoors for house-training. As the dog gets older, he can be more tolerant of deviations in his feeding and relief schedule.

yourself why you want a Pharaoh, whether purely as a pet or as a show dog, or as a participant in other areas of the dog sport. This should be made clear to the breeder when you make your initial inquiries, for you will certainly need to take the breeder's advice as to which available puppy displays the most promise for your endeavors. If looking for a pet, you should discuss your family situation with the breeder, and again take his advice as to which puppy is likely to suit you best.

Watch the puppies interact together, and see which little personality appeals to you most,

Even at eight weeks old, the alert and intelligent nature of the Pharaoh Hound is evident in this pup's expressive face.

obviously also taking into account the overall quality of the dog, especially if destined for a show home. Never be tempted to take pity on an unduly shy puppy; in doing so, you will be asking for trouble in the long term, as such a dog is likely to encounter problems in socializing.

You should have done plenty of background homework on the breed, and preferably have visited a few breed club or all-breed shows, giving you an opportunity to see the breed in some numbers. This will have provided you with the chance to see the dogs with their breeders and owners, so you can give thought to which people's stock you most appreciate and can make some contacts in the breed.

Remember that the dog you select should remain with you for the duration of his life, which is usually around 14 years, sometimes longer, so making the right decision from the outset is of utmost importance. No dog should be moved from one home to another simply because his owners were not considerate enough to have done sufficient research before selecting the breed. It is always important to remember that, when looking for a puppy, a good breeder will be assessing you as a prospective new owner just as carefully as you are selecting the breeder.

ARE YOU PREPARED?

Unfortunately, when a puppy is bought by someone who does not take into consideration the time and attention that dog ownership requires, it is the puppy who suffers when he is either abandoned or placed in a shelter by a frustrated owner. So all of the "homework" you do in preparation for your pup's arrival will benefit you both. The more informed you are, the more you will know what to expect and the better equipped you will be to handle the ups and downs of raising a puppy. Hopefully, everyone in the household is willing to do his part in raising and caring for the pup. The anticipation of owning a dog often brings a lot of promises from excited family members: "I will walk him every day," "I will feed him," "I will house-train him," etc., but these things take time and effort, and promises can easily be forgotten once the novelty of the new pet has worn off.

Puppies almost invariably look enchanting, but you must select one from a caring breeder who has given the puppies all the attention they deserve and has looked after them well. It is important for breeders to socialize puppies as early as possible, and the results of this socialization should be apparent when you meet the puppies.

The puppy you select should look well fed, but not pot-bellied, as this might indicate worms. Eyes should look bright and clear, without discharge. The nose should be moist, an indication of good health, but should never be runny. It goes without saying that there should certainly be no evidence of loose motions or of parasites. The puppy you choose should also have a healthy-looking coat, an important indicator of good health internally.

Something else to consider is whether or not to take out veterinary insurance. Vet's bills can mount up, and you must always be certain that sufficient funds are available to give your dog any veterinary attention that may be needed. The range of policies is becoming more extensive as this type of insurance grows in popularity.

PUPPY APPEARANCE

Your puppy should have a well-fed appearance but not a distended abdomen, which may indicate worms or incorrect feeding, or both. The body should be firm, with a solid feel. The skin of the abdomen should be pale pink and clean, without signs of scratching or rash. Check the legs to see if the dewclaws were removed, as this is done at only a few days old.

COMMITMENT OF OWNERSHIP

After considering all of these factors, you have most likely already made some very important decisions about selecting your puppy. You have chosen the Pharaoh Hound, which means that you have decided which characteristics you want in a dog and what type of dog will best fit into your family and lifestyle. If you have selected a breeder, you have gone a step further—you have done your research and found a responsible, conscientious person who breeds quality Pharaohs and who should be a reliable source of help as you and your puppy adjust to life together. If you have observed a litter in action, you have obtained a firsthand look at the dynamics of a puppy pack and, thus, you should learn about each pup's individual personality—perhaps you have even found one that particularly appeals to you.

However, even if you have not yet found the Pharaoh puppy of your dreams, observing pups will help you learn to recognize certain behavior and to determine what a pup's behavior indicates about his temperament. You will be able to pick out which pups are outgoing, confident, shy, playful, friendly, dominant, etc. Equally as important, you will learn to recognize what a healthy

pup should look and act like. All of these things will help you in your search, and when you find the Pharaoh Hound that was meant for you, you will know it!

Researching your breed, selecting a responsible breeder and observing as many pups as possible are all important steps on the way to dog ownership. It may seem like a lot of effort...and you have not even taken the pup home yet! Remember, though, you cannot be too careful when it comes to deciding on the type of dog you want and finding out about your prospective pup's background. Buying a puppy is not—or *should* not be—just another whimsical purchase. This is one instance in which you actually do get to choose your own family! You may be thinking that buying a puppy should be fun—it should not be so serious and so much work. Keep in mind

When visiting a breeder, ask to see all of the dogs on the premises and visit their living quarters. This will give you an idea of how well the dogs are cared for and how dogs of that particular line mature.

INHERIT THE MIND

In order to know whether or not a puppy will fit into your lifestyle, you need to assess his personality. A good way to do this is to interact with his parents. Your pup inherits not only his appearance but also his personality and temperament from the sire and dam. If the parents are fearful or overly aggressive, these same traits may likely show up in your puppy.

that your puppy is not a cuddly stuffed toy or decorative lawn ornament, but a creature that will become a real member of your family. You will come to realize that, while buying a puppy is a pleasurable and exciting endeavor, it is not something to be taken lightly. Relax...the fun will start when the pup comes home!

Always keep in mind that a puppy is nothing more than a baby in a puppy-dog disguise...a baby who is virtually helpless in a human world and who trusts his owner for fulfillment of his basic needs for survival. In addition to food, water and shelter, your pup needs care, protection, guidance and love. If you are not prepared to commit to this, then you are not prepared to own a dog of any breed.

"Wait a minute," you say. "How hard could this be? All of my neighbors own dogs and they seem to be doing just fine. Why should I have to worry about all of this?" Well, you should not worry about it; in fact, you will probably find that once your Pharaoh pup gets used to his new home, he will fall into his place in the family quite naturally. But it never hurts to emphasize the commitment of dog ownership. With some time and patience, it is really not too difficult to raise a curious and lovable Pharaoh pup to be a well-adjusted and well-mannered adult dog—a dog that could be your most loyal friend.

PUPPY PERSONALITY

When a litter becomes available to you, choosing a pup out of all those adorable faces will not be an easy task! Sound temperament is of utmost importance, but each pup has its own personality and some may be better suited to you than others. A feisty, independent pup will do well in a home with older children and adults, while quiet, shy puppies will thrive in homes with minimal noise and distractions. Your breeder knows the pups best and should be able to guide you in the right direction.

PREPARING PUPPY'S PLACE IN YOUR HOME

Researching your breed and finding a breeder are only two aspects of the homework you will have to do before taking your Pharaoh puppy home. You will also have to prepare your home and family for the new addition. Much as you would prepare a nursery for a newborn baby, you will need to designate a place in your home that will be the puppy's own. How you prepare your home will depend on how much freedom the dog will be allowed. Whatever you decide, you must ensure that he has a place that he can call his own.

When you bring your new puppy into your home, you are bringing him into what will become his home as well. Obviously, you did not buy a puppy so that he could take control of your home, but in order for a puppy to grow into a stable, well-adjusted dog, he has to feel comfortable in his surroundings. Remember, he is leaving the warmth and security of his mother and littermates, as well as the familiarity of the only place he has ever known, so it is important to make his transition as easy as possible. By preparing a place in your home for the puppy, you are making him feel as welcome as possible in a strange new place. It should not take him long to get used to it, but the sudden shock of being transplanted is somewhat traumatic for a young pup. Imagine how a small child would feel in the same

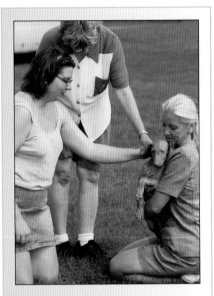

"YOU BETTER SHOP AROUND!"

Finding a reputable breeder who sells healthy pups is very important, but make sure that the breeder you choose is not only someone you respect but also someone with whom you feel comfortable. Your breeder will be a resource long after you buy your puppy, and you must be able to call with reasonable questions without being made to feel like a pest! If you don't connect on a personal level, investigate some other breeders before making a final decision.

situation—that is how your puppy must be feeling. It is up to you to reassure him and to let him know, "Little fellow, you are going to like it here!"

Your local pet shop will have a variety of crates. Choose one from the outset that will be large enough for your Pharaoh Hound when the dog is fully grown.

PHOTO COURTESY OF DOSKOCIL.

WHAT YOU SHOULD BUY

CRATE

To someone unfamiliar with the use of crates in dog training, it may seem like punishment to shut a dog in a crate, but this is not the case at all. More and more breeders and trainers around the world are recommending crates as preferred tools for show puppies and pet puppies alike. Crates are not cruel—crates have many humane and highly effective uses in dog care and training. For example, crate

training is a very popular and very successful house-training method, a crate can keep your dog safe during travel and, perhaps most importantly, a crate provides your dog with a place of his own in your home. It serves as a "doggie bedroom" of sorts— your Pharaoh Hound can curl up

PEDIGREE VS. REGISTRATION CERTIFICATE

Too often new owners are confused between these two important documents. Your puppy's pedigree, essentially a family tree, is a written record of a dog's genealogy of three generations or more. The pedigree will show you the names as well as performance titles of all dogs in your pup's background. Your breeder must provide you with a registration application, with his part properly filled out. You must complete the application and send it to the AKC with the proper fee. Every puppy must come from a litter that has been AKC-registered by the breeder, born in the USA and from a sire and dam that are also registered with the AKC.

The seller must provide you with complete records to identify the puppy. The AKC requires that the seller provide the buyer with the following: breed; sex, color and markings; date of birth; litter number (when available); names and registration numbers of the parents; breeder's name; and date sold or delivered.

in his crate when he wants to sleep or when he just needs a break. Many dogs sleep in their crates overnight. With soft bedding and his favorite toy, a crate becomes a cozy pseudo-den for your dog. Like his ancestors, he too will seek out the comfort and retreat of a den—you just happen to be providing him with something a little more luxurious than what his early ancestors enjoyed.

As far as purchasing a crate, the type that you buy is up to you. It will most likely be one of the two most popular types: wire or fiberglass. There are advantages and disadvantages to each type. For example, a wire crate is more open, allowing the air to flow through and affording the dog a view of what is going on around him, while a fiberglass crate is sturdier. Both can double as travel crates, providing protection for the dog in the car.

The size of the crate is another thing to consider. Puppies do not stay puppies forever—in fact, sometimes it seems as if they grow right before your eyes. A small crate may be fine for a very young Pharaoh pup, but it will not do him much good for long! Unless you have the money and the inclination to buy a new crate every time your pup has a growth spurt, it is better to get one that will accommodate your dog both as a

CRATE-TRAINING TIPS

During crate training, you should partition off the section of the crate in which the pup stays. If he is given too big an area, this will hinder your training efforts. Crate training is based on the fact that a dog does not like to soil his sleeping quarters, so it is ineffective to keep a pup in an area that is so big that he can eliminate in one end and get far enough away from it to sleep. Also, you want to make the crate den-like for the pup. Blankets and a favorite toy will make the crate cozy for the small pup; as he grows, you may want to evict some of his "roommates" to make more room. It will take some coaxing at first, but be patient. Given some time to get used to it, your pup will adapt to his new home-within-a-home quite nicely.

PET INSURANCE

Just like you can insure your car, your house and your own health, you likewise can insure your dog's health. Investigate a pet insurance policy by talking to your vet. Depending on the age of your dog, the breed and the kind of coverage you desire, your policy can be very affordable. Most policies cover accidental injuries, poisoning and thousands of medical problems and illnesses, including cancers. Some carriers also offer routine care and immunization coverage.

pup and at full size. A large-size crate will be necessary for a full-grown Pharaoh, who stands approximately 25 inches high, but whose ears make him "stand" as high as 36 inches!

BEDDING

A nice crate pad and a blanket in the dog's crate will help the dog feel more at home. This will take the place of the leaves, twigs, etc., that the pup would use in

The pups in the litter should be curious about visitors and eager to meet you. This is a good indication of stable temperament and early socialization.

the wild to make a den; the pup can make his own "burrow" in the crate. Although your pup is far removed from his den-making ancestors, the denning instinct is still a part of his genetic makeup. Second, until you take your pup home, he has been sleeping amid the warmth of his dam and littermates, and while a blanket is not the same as a warm, breathing body, it still provides heat and something with which to snuggle. You will want to wash your pup's bedding frequently in case he has an accident in his crate, and replace or remove any blanket or padding that becomes ragged and starts to fall apart.

TOYS

Toys are a must for dogs of all ages, especially for curious playful pups. Puppies are the children of the dog world, and what child does not love toys? Chew toys provide enjoyment for both dog and owner—your dog will enjoy playing with his favorite toys, while you will enjoy the fact that they distract him from your expensive shoes and leather sofa. Puppies love to chew; in fact, chewing is a physical need for pups as they are teething, and everything looks appetizing! The full range of your possessions—from your favorite slipper to your new Persian carpet—are fair game in the eyes of a teething pup.

Puppies are not all that discerning when it comes to finding something to literally "sink their teeth into"— everything tastes great! As youngsters, Pharaoh Hounds are often aggressive chewers, but they eventually grow out of this.

They like balls, but these should be of suitable size for the puppy or adult (too small and it could be swallowed). Hard nylon or plastic chews are also suitable. Always take care when giving squeaky toys, for Pharaoh Hounds will usually remove squeaks and eyes immediately! If a pup "disembowels" one of these, the small plastic squeaker inside can be dangerous if swallowed.

Monitor the condition of all your pup's toys carefully and get rid of any that have been chewed to the point of becoming potentially dangerous. Always provide your Pharaoh Hound, puppy or adult, with the safest, most durable toys.

Breeders advise owners also to resist stuffed toys, because they can become de-stuffed in no time. The overly excited pup may ingest the stuffing, which is neither digestible nor nutritious. Be careful of natural bones, which have a tendency to splinter into sharp, dangerous pieces. Also be careful of rawhide, which can turn into pieces that are easy to swallow and become a mushy mess on your carpet.

TOYS, TOYS, TOYS!

With a big variety of dog toys available, and so many that look like they would be a lot of fun for a dog, be careful in your selection. It is amazing what a set of puppy teeth can do to an innocent-looking toy, so, obviously, safety is a major consideration. Be sure to choose the most durable products that you can find. Hard nylon bones and toys are a safe bet, and many of them are offered in different scents and flavors that will be sure to capture your dog's attention. It is always fun to play a game of fetch with your dog, and there are balls and flying discs that are specially made to withstand dog teeth.

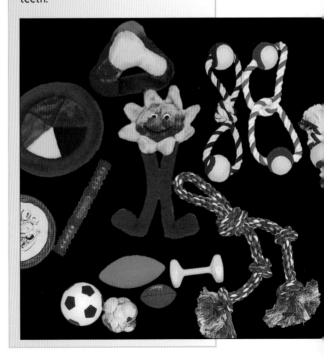

Choose a lightweight collar for your puppy and accustom him to it when he is young. Be sure that the collar can be adjusted as the puppy grows.

purposes, the nylon leash is a good choice.

As your pup grows up and gets used to walking on the leash, and can do it politely, you may want to purchase a flexible leash. These leashes allow you to extend or retract the length of the leash. Be sure that your Pharaoh Hound falls within the flexible lead's weight limits.

COLLAR

Your pup should get used to wearing a collar all the time since you will want to attach his ID tags to it. Plus, you have to attach the leash to something! A lightweight nylon collar is a good choice; make sure that it fits snugly enough so that the pup cannot wriggle out of it, but is loose enough so that it will not be uncomfortably tight around the

LEASH

A nylon leash is probably the best option, as it is the most resistant to puppy teeth should your pup take a liking to chewing on his leash. Of course, this is a habit that should be nipped in the bud, but, if your pup likes to chew on his leash, he has a very slim chance of being able to chew through the strong nylon. Nylon leashes are also lightweight, which is good for a young Pharaoh who is just getting used to the idea of walking on a leash. For everyday walking and safety

FINANCIAL RESPONSIBILITY

Grooming tools, collars, leashes, s crate, a dog bed and, of course, toys will be expenses to you when you first obtain your pup, and the cost will continue throughout your dog's lifetime. If your puppy damages or destroys your possessions (as most puppies surely will!) or something belonging to a neighbor, you can calculate additional expense. There is also flea and pest control, which every dog owner faces more than once. You must be able to handle the financial responsibility of owning a dog.

CHOOSE AN APPROPRIATE COLLAR

The **BUCKLE COLLAR** is the standard collar used for everyday purposes. Be sure that you adjust the buckle on growing puppies. Check it every day. It can become too tight overnight! These collars can be made of leather or nylon. Attach your dog's identification tags to this collar.

The **CHOKE COLLAR** is designed for training. It is constructed of highly polished steel so that it slides easily through the stainless steel loop. The idea is that the dog controls the pressure around his neck and he will stop pulling if the collar becomes uncomfortable. It should *never* be left on a dog when not training.

The **HALTER** is for a trained dog that has to be restrained to prevent running away, chasing a cat and the like. Considered the most humane of all collars, it is frequently used on smaller dogs on which collars are not comfortable.

Your local pet shop sells an array of dishes and bowls for water and food.

PHOTO COURTESY OF MIKKI PET PRODUCTS.

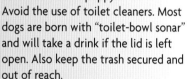

SKULL & CROSSBONES

Thoroughly puppy-proof your house before bringing your puppy home. Never use cockroach or rodent poisons or plant fertilizers in any area accessible to the puppy.

Avoid the use of toilet cleaners. Most dogs are born with "toilet-bowl sonar" and will take a drink if the lid is left open. Also keep the trash secured and out of reach.

Scour your garage for potential puppy dangers. Remove weed killers, pesticides and antifreeze materials. Antifreeze is highly toxic and just a few drops can kill a puppy or an adult dog. The sweet taste attracts the animal, who will quickly consume it from the floor or pavement.

pup's neck. You should be able to fit a finger between the pup and the collar. It may take some time for your pup to get used to wearing the collar, but soon he will not even notice that it is there. Choke collars are made for training, but should only be used by an experienced handler. The martingale is a gentler "check" collar that is also an effective training collar for the Pharaoh Hound.

FOOD AND WATER BOWLS

Your pup will need two bowls, one for food and one for water. You may want two sets of bowls, one for inside and one for outside, depending on where the dog will be fed and where he will be spending time. Stainless steel or sturdy plastic bowls are popular choices. Plastic bowls are more chewable. Dogs tend not to chew on the steel variety, which can be sterilized. It is important to buy sturdy bowls since anything is in danger of being chewed by puppy teeth and you do not want your dog to be constantly chewing apart his bowl (for his safety and for your wallet!).

It is your responsibility to clean up after your dog has relieved himself. Pet shops have various aids to assist in the cleanup job.

CLEANING SUPPLIES
Until a pup is house-trained, you will be doing a lot of cleaning. Accidents will occur, which is acceptable in the beginning because the puppy does not know any better. All you can do is be prepared to clean up any accidents. Old rags, towels, newspapers and a safe disinfectant are good to have on hand.

BEYOND THE BASICS
The items previously discussed are the bare necessities. You will find out what else you need as you go along—grooming supplies, flea/tick protection, baby gates to partition a room, etc. These things will vary depending on your situation, but it is important that you have everything you need to feed and make your Pharaoh Hound comfortable in his first few days at home.

PUPPY-PROOFING YOUR HOME
Aside from making sure that your Pharaoh will be comfortable in your home, you also have to make sure that your home is safe for your Pharaoh. This means taking precautions that your pup will not get into anything he should not get into and that there is nothing within his reach that may harm him should he sniff it, chew it, inspect it, etc. This probably seems obvious since, while you are primarily concerned with your pup's safety, at the same time you do not want your belongings to be ruined. Breakables should be placed out of reach if your dog is to have

NATURAL TOXINS

Examine your grass and landscaping before bringing your puppy home. Many varieties of plants have leaves, stems or flowers that are toxic if ingested, and you can depend on a curious puppy to investigate them.

If you see your dog carrying a piece of vegetation in his mouth, approach him in a quiet, disinterested manner, avoid eye contact, pet him and gradually remove the plant from his mouth. Alternatively, offer him a treat and maybe he'll drop the plant on his own accord. Be sure no toxic plants are growing in your own yard or kept in your home. Ask your vet for information on poisonous plants or research them at your library.

full run of the house. If he is to be limited to certain places within the house, keep any potentially dangerous items in the "off-limits" areas. An electrical cord can pose a danger should the puppy decide to taste it—and who is going to convince a pup that it would not make a great chew toy? Cords should be fastened tightly against the wall, out of the reach of the puppy. If your dog is going to spend time in a crate, make sure that there is nothing near his crate that he can reach if he sticks his curious little nose or paws through the openings. Just as you would with a child, keep all household cleaners and chemicals where the pup cannot reach them.

It is also important to make sure that the outside of your home is safe. Of course, your puppy should never be unsupervised, but a pup let loose in the yard will want to run and explore, and he should be granted that freedom. Do not let a fence give you a false sense of security; you would be surprised how crafty (and persistent) a Pharaoh Hound can be in figuring out how to dig under and squeeze his way through small holes, or to jump or climb over a fence.

Remember that this breed is talented at escaping! The remedy is to make the fence well embedded into the ground and high enough so that it really is impossible for your dog to get over it (about 6 feet should suffice). Be sure to secure any gaps in the fence. Check the fence periodically to ensure that it is in good shape and make repairs as needed; a very determined pup may return to the same spot to "work on it" until he is able to get through.

FIRST TRIP TO THE VET

You have selected your puppy, and your home and family are ready. Now all you have to do is collect your Pharaoh from the breeder and the fun begins, right? Well…not so fast. Something else you need to prepare is your pup's first trip to the vet. Perhaps the breeder can recommend someone in the area who specializes in sighthounds, or maybe you know

some other Pharaoh owners who can suggest a good vet. Either way, you should have an appointment arranged for your pup before you pick him up.

The pup's first visit will consist of an overall examination to make sure that the pup does not have any problems that are not apparent to you. The vet will also set up a schedule for the pup's vaccinations; the breeder will inform you of which ones the pup has already received and the vet can continue from there.

INTRODUCTION TO THE FAMILY

Everyone in the house will be excited about the puppy's coming home and will want to pet him and play with him, but it is best to make the introductions low-key so as not to overwhelm the puppy. He is apprehensive already. It is the first time he has been separated from his dam and

Keep in mind that pups do much investigating with their mouths, so always supervise your pup's explorations indoors and out.

HOW VACCINES WORK

If you've just bought a puppy, you surely know the importance of having your pup vaccinated, but do you understand how vaccines work? Vaccines contain the same bacteria or viruses that cause the disease you want to prevent, but they have been chemically modified so that they don't cause any harm. Instead, the vaccine causes your dog to produce antibodies that fight the harmful bacteria. Thus, if your dog is exposed to the disease in the future, the antibodies will destroy the viruses or bacteria.

PLAY'S THE THING

Teaching the puppy to play with his toys in running and fetching games is an ideal way to help the puppy develop muscle, learn motor skills and bond with you, his owner and master. He also needs to learn how to inhibit his bite reflex and never to use his teeth on people, forbidden objects and other animals in play. Whenever you play with your puppy, you make the rules. This becomes an important message to your puppy in teaching him that you are the pack leader and control everything he does in life. Once your dog accepts you as his leader, your relationship with him will be cemented for life.

the breeder, and the ride to your home is likely to be the first time he has been in a car. The last thing you want to do is smother him, as this will only frighten him further. This is not to say that human contact is not extremely necessary at this stage, because this is the time when a connection between the pup and his human family is formed. Gentle petting and soothing words should help console him, as well as just putting him down and letting him explore on his own (under your watchful eye, of course).

The pup may approach the family members or may busy himself with exploring for a while. Gradually, each person should spend some time with the pup, one at a time, crouching down to get as close to the pup's level as possible while letting him sniff their hands and petting him gently. He definitely needs human attention and he needs to be touched—this is how to form an immediate bond. Just remember that the pup is experiencing a lot of things for the first time, at the same time. There are new people, new noises, new smells and new things to investigate, so be gentle, be affectionate and be as comforting as you can.

PUP'S FIRST NIGHT HOME

You have traveled home with your new charge safely in his

FEEDING TIPS

You will probably start feeding your pup the same food that he has been getting from the breeder; the breeder should give you a few days' supply to start you off. Although you should not give your pup too many treats, you will want to have puppy treats on hand for coaxing, training, rewards, etc. Be careful, though, as a small pup's calorie requirements are relatively low and a few treats can add up to almost a full day's worth of calories without the required nutrition.

crate or on a friend or family member's lap. He's been to the vet for a thorough check-up; he's been weighed, his papers examined; perhaps he's even been vaccinated and wormed as well. He's met the family, including the excited children and the less-than-happy cat. He's explored his area, his new bed, the yard and anywhere else he's been permitted. He's eaten his first meal at home and relieved himself in the proper place. He's heard lots of new sounds, smelled new friends and seen more of the outside world than ever before.

That was just the first day! He's worn out and is ready for bed...or so you think!

It's puppy's first night and you are ready to say "Good night." Keep in mind that this is puppy's first night ever to be sleeping alone. His dam and littermates are no longer at paw's length and he's a bit scared, cold and lonely. Be reassuring to your new family member, this is not the time to spoil him and give in to his inevitable whining.

Puppies whine. They whine to let others know where they are and hopefully to get company out of it. Place your pup in his new bed or crate in his room and close the door. Mercifully, he may fall asleep without a peep. When the inevitable occurs, ignore the whining: he is fine. Be strong and keep his interest in mind. Do not allow yourself to feel guilty and visit the pup. He will fall asleep eventually.

Many breeders recommend placing a piece of bedding from his former home in his new bed so that he recognizes the scent of his littermates. Others still advise placing a hot water bottle in his

Puppies' natural instincts can be developed through play. These future coursers are eagerly chasing a feather on a long stick.

PREVENTING PUPPY PROBLEMS

SOCIALIZATION

Now that you have done all of the preparatory work and have helped your pup get accustomed to his new home and family, it is about time for you to have some fun! Socializing your Pharaoh Hound pup gives you the opportunity to show off your new friend, and your pup gets to reap the benefits of being an adorable, intriguing creature that people will want to pet and, in general, think is absolutely precious!

Besides getting to know his new family, your puppy should be exposed to other people, animals and situations. Pharaoh Hounds are more timid and reserved than many breeds, so it is extremely important to begin socialization right away.

What better way to make a Pharaoh Hound pup feel right at home than to surround him with designs reminiscent of his heritage?

bed for warmth. This latter may be a good idea, provided the pup doesn't attempt to suckle—he'll get good and wet and may not fall asleep so fast.

Puppy's first night can be somewhat stressful for the pup and his new family. Remember that you are setting the tone of nighttime at your house. Unless you want to play with your pup every night at 10 p.m., midnight and 2 a.m., don't initiate the habit. Your family will thank you, and soon so will your pup!

STRESS-FREE
Some experts in canine health advise that stress during a dog's early years of development can compromise and weaken his immune system, and may trigger the potential for a shortened life. They emphasize the need for happy and stress-free growing-up years.

THE COCOA WARS

Chocolate contains the chemical thebromine, which is poisonous to dogs, although "chocolates" especially made for dogs are safe (as they don't actually contain chocolate) but not recommended. Any item that encourages your dog to enjoy the taste of cocoa should be discouraged. You should also exercise caution when using mulch in your garden. This frequently contains cocoa hulls, and dogs have been known to die from eating the mulch.

Socialization will help him become well adjusted as he grows up and less prone to being timid or fearful of the new things he will encounter. Your pup's social-ization began with the breeder, but now it is your responsibility to continue it. The socialization he receives up until the age of 12 weeks is the most critical, as this is the time when he forms his impressions of the outside world. Be especially careful during the eight-to-ten-week-old period, also known as the fear period. The interaction he receives during this time should be gentle and reassuring. Lack of socialization can manifest itself in fear and aggression as the dog grows up. He needs lots of human contact,

affection, handling and exposure to other animals.

Once your pup has arrived at his new home, feel free to take him out and about (on his lead, of course). Walk him around the neighborhood, take him on your daily errands, let people pet him, let him meet other dogs and pets, etc. Puppies do not have to try to make friends; there will be no shortage of people who will want to introduce themselves. Just make sure that you carefully supervise each meeting. If the neighborhood children want to say hello, for example, that is great—children and pups most often make great companions. However, sometimes an excited child can unintentionally handle a pup too roughly, or an overzealous pup can playfully nip a little too hard. You want to

It's mom's job to let the pups know when they're out of line. This is the pups' earliest form of education.

experience with a child may grow up to be a dog that is shy around or aggressive toward children.

CONSISTENCY IN TRAINING

Dogs, being pack animals, naturally need a leader, or else they try to establish dominance in their packs. When you welcome a dog into your family, the choice of who becomes the leader and who becomes the pack is entirely up to you! Your pup's intuitive quest for dominance, coupled with the fact that it is nearly impossible to look at an adorable Pharaoh pup with his lopsided ears and not cave in, give the pup almost an unfair advantage in getting the upper hand!

A pup will definitely test the waters to see what he can and cannot do. Do not give in to those pleading eyes—stand your ground when it comes to disciplining the pup and make sure that all family members do the same. It will only confuse the pup when Mother tells him to get off the sofa when he is used to sitting up there with Father to watch the nightly news. Avoid discrepancies by having all members of the household decide on the rules before the pup even comes home...and be consistent in enforcing them! Early training shapes the dog's personality, so you cannot be unclear in what you expect.

MANNERS MATTER

During the socialization process, a puppy should meet people, experience different environments and definitely be exposed to other canines. Through playing and interacting with other dogs, your puppy will learn lessons, ranging from controlling the pressure of his jaws by biting his littermates to the inner-workings of the canine pack that he will apply to his human relationships for the rest of his life. That is why removing a puppy from his litter too early (before eight weeks) can be detrimental to the pup's development.

make socialization experiences positive ones. What a pup learns during this very formative stage will affect his attitude toward future encounters. You want your dog to be comfortable around everyone. A pup that has a bad

COMMON PUPPY PROBLEMS

The best way to prevent puppy problems is to be proactive in stopping an undesirable behavior as soon as it starts. The old saying "You can't teach an old dog new tricks" does not necessarily hold true, but it is true that it *is* much easier to discourage bad behavior in a young developing pup than to wait until the pup's bad behavior becomes the adult dog's bad habit. There are some problems that are especially prevalent in puppies as they develop.

NIPPING

As puppies start to teethe, they feel the need to sink their teeth into anything available...unfortunately that includes your fingers, arms, hair and toes. You may find this behavior cute for the first five seconds...until you feel just how sharp those puppy teeth are. This is something you want to discourage immediately and consistently with a firm "No!" (or whatever number of firm "Nos" it takes for him to understand that you mean business). Then replace your finger with an appropriate chew toy. While this behavior is merely annoying when the dog is young, it can become dangerous as your Pharaoh's adult teeth grow in and his jaws develop if he thinks it is okay to nip and nibble on his human friends. Your Pharaoh Hound does not

mean any harm with a friendly nip, but he also does not know his own strength.

CRYING/WHINING

Your pup will often cry, whine, whimper, howl or make some type of commotion when he is left alone. This is basically his way of calling out for attention to make sure that you know he is there and that you have not forgotten about him. He feels insecure when he is left alone,

Begin with a sound puppy and teach him to live by your rules, and you'll be rewarded with a dog that you'll be delighted to live with.

when you are out of the house and he is in his crate or when you are in another part of the house and he cannot see you. The noise he is making is an expres-

CHEWING TIPS

Chewing goes hand in hand with nipping in the sense that a teething puppy is always looking for a way to soothe his aching gums. In this case, instead of chewing on you, he may have taken a liking to your favorite shoe or something else that he should not be chewing. Again, realize that this is a normal canine behavior that does not need to be discouraged, only redirected. Your pup just needs to be taught what is acceptable to chew on and what is off-limits. Consistently tell him "No!" when you catch him chewing on something forbidden and give him a chew toy.

Conversely, praise him when you catch him chewing on something appropriate. In this way, you are discouraging the inappropriate behavior and reinforcing the desired behavior. The puppy's chewing should stop after his adult teeth have come in, but an adult dog continues to chew for various reasons—perhaps because he is bored, needs to relieve tension or just likes to chew. That is why it is important to redirect his chewing when he is still young.

sion of the anxiety he feels at being alone, so he needs to be taught that being alone is okay. You are not actually training the dog to stop making noise, you are training him to feel comfortable when he is alone and thus removing the need for him to make the noise.

This is where the crate with cozy bedding and a toy comes in handy. You want to know that he is safe when you are not there to supervise, and you know that he will be safe in his crate rather than roaming freely about the house. In order for the pup to stay in his crate without making a fuss, he needs to be comfortable in his crate. On that note, it is extremely important that the crate is never used as a form of punishment, or the pup will develop a negative association with the crate.

Accustom the pup to the crate in short, gradually increasing time intervals in which you put him in the crate, maybe with a treat, and stay in the room with him. If he cries or makes a fuss, do not go to him, but stay in his sight. Gradually he will realize that staying in his crate is just fine without your help, and it will not be so traumatic for him when you are not around. You may want to leave the radio on softly when you leave the house; the sound of human voices may be comforting to him.

PHARAOH HOUND

FEEDING THE PHARAOH

A Pharaoh Hound should be fed sensibly on a high-quality diet, but protein content will vary according to whether or not the dog lives an especially active lifestyle. When purchasing a puppy, a carefully selected breeder should be able to give good advice in this regard, but it is generally accepted that dogs leading active lives need more protein than those who spend most of their time by the fireside.

The lean, muscular Pharaoh Hound doesn't have anywhere to hide an extra ounce. Your dog's proper feeding will be evident in his sleek body and luminous coat.

TIPPING THE SCALES

Good nutrition is vital to your dog's health, but many people end up over-feeding or giving unnecessary supplements. Here are some common doggie diet don'ts:

- Adding milk, yogurt and cheese to your dog's diet may seem like a good idea for coat and skin care, but dairy products are very fattening and can cause indigestion.
- Diets high in fat will not cause heart attacks in dogs but will certainly cause your dog to gain weight.
- Most importantly, don't assume your dog will simply stop eating once he doesn't need any more food. Given the chance, he will eat you out of house and home!

An owner should never be tempted to allow his dog to put on too much weight, for an overweight dog is more prone to health problems than one that is of correct weight for his size. Feeding too many treats between meals will not only risk an unhealthy dog, but the additional few pounds will certainly show on the lithe Pharaoh Hound!

Some owners like to feed two meals each day, others just one. However frequently you decide to feed your dog, remember that no dog should ever be fed within at least an hour before or after strenuous exercise. Many owners of longer-legged breeds prefer to offer food in a container that is raised from the ground, a preven-

FEEDING TIPS

- Dog food must be served at room temperature, neither too hot nor too cold. Fresh water, changed often and served in a clean bowl, is mandatory.
- Never feed your dog from the table while you are eating, and never feed your dog leftovers from your own meal. They usually contain too much fat and too much seasoning.
- Dogs must chew their food. Hard pellets are excellent; soups and stews are to be avoided.
- Don't add leftovers or any extras to commercial dog food. The normal food is usually balanced, and adding something extra destroys the balance.
- Except for age-related changes, dogs do not require dietary variations. They can be fed the same diet, day after day, without their becoming bored or ill.

tative method to ward off the potentially fatal condition known as bloat.

There are now numerous high-quality canine foods available, and one of them is sure to suit your hound. Once again, you should be able to obtain sound advice from your dog's breeder as to which food is considered most suitable. When you buy your puppy, the breeder should have provided you with a diet sheet, giving details of exactly how your puppy has been fed. Of course, you will be at liberty to change that food, together with the frequency and timing of meals, as the youngster reaches adulthood, but this should be done gradually.

Some owners prefer to feed fresh food instead of one of the more convenient complete diets, but there are so many of the latter now available, some scientifically balanced, that a lot will depend on personal preference. If you encounter the occasional finicky eater, although you have to be very careful not to unbalance an otherwise balanced diet, sometimes the addition of a little flavored stock, or even gravy, will gain a dog's interest and stimulate the appetite.

TYPES OF FOOD
Today the choices of food for your Pharaoh Hound are many and varied. There are simply dozens

of brands of food in all sorts of flavors and textures, ranging from puppy diets to those for seniors. There are even hypoallergenic and low-calorie diets available. Because your Pharaoh's food has a bearing on coat, health and temperament, it is essential that the most suitable diet is selected for a Pharaoh of his age. It is fair to say, however, that even experi-

There is no better nutrition for pups during their first weeks of life than their mother's milk.

enced owners can be perplexed by the enormous range of foods available. Only understanding what is best for your dog will help you reach an informed decision.

Dog foods are produced in three basic types: dry, semi-moist and canned. Dry foods are useful for the cost-conscious, for overall they tend to be less expensive than semi-moist or canned. They also contain the least fat and the most preservatives. In general, canned foods are made up of 60–70% water, while semi-moist ones often contain so much sugar that they are perhaps the least preferred by owners, even though their dogs seem to like them.

When selecting your dog's diet, three stages of development must be considered: the puppy stage, the adult stage and the senior stage.

PUPPY STAGE
Puppies instinctively want to suck milk from their mother's teats and a normal puppy will exhibit this

THE CANINE GOURMET
Your dog does not prefer a fresh bone. Indeed, he wants it properly aged and, if given such a treat indoors, he is more likely to try to bury it in the carpet than he is to settle in for a good chew! If you have a yard, give him such delicacies outside and guide him to a place suitable for his "bone yard." He will carefully place the treasure in its earthy vault and seemingly forget about it. Trust me, his seeming distaste or lack of thanks for your thoughtfulness is not that at all. He will return in a few days to inspect the bone, perhaps to re-bury it, and, when it is just right, he will relish it as much as you do that cooked-to-perfection steak. If he is in a concrete or bricked kennel run, he will be especially frustrated at the hopelessness of the situation. He will vacillate between ignoring it completely, giving it a few licks to speed the curing process with saliva and trying to hide it behind the water bowl! When the bone has aged a bit, he will set to work on it.

A Worthy Investment

Veterinary studies have proven that a balanced high-quality diet pays off in your dog's coat quality, behavior and activity level. Invest in premium brands for the maximum payoff with your dog.

behavior from just a few moments following birth. If puppies do not attempt to suckle within the first half-hour or so, they should be encouraged to do so by placing them on the nipples, having selected ones with plenty of milk. This early milk supply is important in providing colostrum to protect the puppies during the first eight to ten weeks of their lives. Although a mother's milk is much better than any milk formula, despite there being some excellent ones available, if the puppies do not feed, the breeder will have to feed them himself. For those with less experience, advice from a vet is important so that not only the right quantity of milk but also that of correct quality is fed, at suitably frequent intervals, usually every two hours during the first few days of life.

Puppies should be allowed to nurse from their dam for about the first six weeks, although from the third or fourth week the breeder will begin to introduce small portions of suitable solid food. Most breeders like to introduce alternate milk and meat meals initially, building up to weaning time.

By the time the puppies are seven or a maximum of eight weeks old, they should be fully weaned and fed solely on a proprietary puppy food. Selection of the most suitable, good-quality

diet at this time is essential, for a puppy's fastest growth rate is during the first year of life. Vets are usually able to offer advice in this regard and, although the frequency of meals will be reduced over time, only when a young dog has reached the age of about 15 months should an adult diet be fed. Pharaoh Hounds continue to develop physically until they are three years of age.

Puppy and junior diets should be well balanced for the needs of your dog, so that, except in certain circumstances, additional vitamins, minerals and proteins will not be required.

DO DOGS HAVE TASTE BUDS?

Watching a dog "chow down" enthusiastically leads an owner to wonder whether his dog can taste anything. Yes, dogs have taste buds, with sensory perception of sweet, salty and sour. Puppies are born with fully mature taste buds.

When there's food to be found, leave it to a dog to find it!

ADULT DIETS

A dog is considered an adult when he has stopped growing, so in general the diet of a Pharaoh can be changed to an adult one at about 15 months of age. Again you should rely upon your vet or breeder to recommend an acceptable maintenance diet. Major dog-food manufacturers specialize in this type of food, and it is merely necessary for you to select the one best suited to your dog's needs. As we've mentioned, active dogs have different requirements than more sedentary dogs.

SENIOR DIETS

As dogs get older, their metabolism changes. The older dog usually exercises less, moves more slowly and sleeps more. This change in lifestyle and physiological performance requires a change in diet. Since these changes take place slowly, they might not be recognizable. What is easily recognizable is weight gain. By continuing to feed your dog an adult-maintenance diet when he is slowing down metabolically, your dog will gain weight. Obesity in an older dog compounds the health problems that already accompany old age.

As your dog gets older, few of his organs function up to par. The kidneys slow down and the intestines become less efficient. These age-related factors are best handled with a change in diet and a change in feeding schedule to give smaller portions that are more easily digested.

There is no single best diet for every older dog. While many dogs do well on light or senior diets, other dogs do better on puppy

GRAIN-BASED DIETS

Some less expensive dog foods are based on grains and other plant proteins. While these products may appear to be attractively priced, many breeders prefer a diet based on animal proteins and believe that they are more conducive to your dog's health. Many grain-based diets rely on soy protein, which may cause flatulence (passing gas).

There are many cases, however, when your dog might require a special diet. These special requirements should only be recommended by your veterinarian.

diets or special premium diets such as lamb and rice. Be sensitive to your senior Pharaoh's diet and this will help control other problems that may arise with your old friend.

WATER
Just as your dog needs proper nutrition from his food, water is an essential "nutrient" as well. Water keeps the dog's body properly hydrated and promotes normal function of the body's systems. During housebreaking, it is necessary to keep an eye on how much water your Pharaoh is drinking. Once he is reliably trained he should have access to clean fresh water at all times, although you should limit your Pharaoh's water intake at mealtimes and *never* allow him to gulp water at any time. These are important daily precautions in preventing bloat. Make certain that the dog's water bowl is clean, and change the water often.

EXERCISE
The Pharaoh Hound is a highly active dog, so exercise is necessary for his health, happiness and mental stimulation. Daily exercise is important, and most Pharaoh Hounds will accept as much as they are given! While leash work is also important, it is essential that some of the daily exercise program gives the hound an opportunity to

run free so as to stretch his limbs, as well as to release pent-up energy. Free runs should, of course, only be allowed in places that are completely safe, so all possible escape routes should be thoroughly checked out before letting a dog off-leash.

After exercise, the Pharaoh Hound should be allowed to settle down quietly for a rest, and please remember that, following exercise, at least one full hour should always be allowed before feeding. Puppies should have only limited exercise during the crucial period of bone growth, so young dogs should be exercised with care.

Because Pharaoh Hounds are accomplished escapologists, it goes without saying that the yard and run areas must be completely dog-proof, and the perimeters

Raised bowls for food and water reduce the risk of the dog's swallowing air when he eats and drinks. This is important in protecting the deep-chested Pharaoh against the potentially deadly bloat/gastric torsion.

must be checked regularly to be sure that the Pharaoh is not working on a new exit route, likely by means of digging or chewing through a fence.

GROOMING

COAT CARE AND BATHING

Pharaoh Hounds need little grooming and are generally clean dogs, virtually free from doggy odors. Bathing is only needed occasionally and, when selecting a shampoo, take into consideration that some Pharaohs have a reaction to insecticides. If ever a product used on the coat causes skin irritation, stop using it immediately and change to one that is mild.

Even when showing a Pharaoh Hound, little grooming is required. A light brush (not metal or wire), a rubber or a sisal mitt will remove dead hair, then you

On the move! The graceful Pharaoh Hound is quite a joy to watch in action, and he will revel in the opportunity to stretch his long legs off-lead in a secure area.

DRINK, DRANK, DRUNK—MAKE IT A DOUBLE

In both humans and dogs, as well as other living organisms, water forms the major part of nearly every body tissue. Naturally, we take water for granted, but without it, life as we know it would cease.

For dogs, water is needed to keep their bodies functioning biochemically. Additionally, water is needed to replace the water lost while panting. Unlike humans, who are able to sweat to dissipate heat, dogs must pant to cool down, thereby losing the vital water that their bodies need to regulate their body temperatures. Humans lose electrolyte-containing products and other body-fluid components through sweating; dogs do not lose anything except water.

Water is essential always, but especially so when the weather is hot or humid or when your dog is exercising or working vigorously.

can go over the coat with a hound glove to put the finishing touch. Hound gloves do vary, but a useful one is chamois leather on one side and velvet on the other. A good wipe-over with the chamois side, and then with the velvet one, produces a nice sheen on the coat and is good stimulation for the skin. In between baths, it can be useful to give the hound a wipe-down with a damp cloth, but never leave a dog damp in cold weather or in a draft.

Bathing as needed is important for healthy skin and clean, shiny coat. Again, like most anything, if you accustom your pup to being bathed as a puppy, it will be second nature by the time he grows up. You want your dog to be at ease in the bath or else it could end up a wet, soapy, messy ordeal for both of you!

Brush your Pharaoh Hound thoroughly before wetting his coat. This will get rid of most dead hair and debris. Make certain that your dog has a good non-slip surface to stand on. Begin by wetting the dog's coat. A shower or hose attachment is necessary for thoroughly wetting and rinsing the coat. Check the water temperature to make sure that it is neither too hot nor too cold.

Next, apply shampoo to the dog's coat and work it into a good lather. You should purchase a shampoo that is made for dogs. Do not use a product made for human hair. Wash the head last; you do not want shampoo to drip into the dog's eyes while you are washing the rest of his body. Work the shampoo all the way down to the skin. You can use this opportunity to check the skin for any bumps, bites or other abnormalities. Do not neglect any area of the body— get all of the hard-to-reach places.

Once the dog has been thoroughly shampooed, he

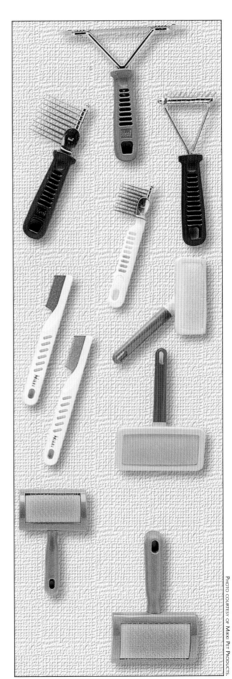

The Pharaoh Hound requires only basic grooming to keep his naturally beautiful short coat in top condition. All of the tools you will need should be available at your local pet shop.

Left: Spraying the coat with a light conditioner adds to the coat's natural sheen. Right: Brushing the coat can be done with a bristle grooming mitt or similar light brush. Below: Don't forget any area of the dog! Even the short hair on the tail needs a little attention.

requires an equally thorough rinsing. Shampoo left in the coat can be irritating to the skin. Protect his eyes from the shampoo by shielding them with your hand and directing the flow of water in the opposite direction. You should also avoid getting water in the ear canal. Be prepared for your dog to shake out his coat—you might want to stand back, but make sure you have a hold on the dog to keep him from running through the house, and have a heavy towel ready.

EAR CARE

It is always necessary to keep a dog's ears clean, and this is especially important in the case of the Pharaoh Hound, which has such large ears. Ears should be kept clean using a special cleaner, but take care never to probe into the ear canal, as this might cause injury.

NAILS

Never forget that toenails should be kept short. How frequently the nails will need to be clipped will depend on how often the dog walks on hard surfaces, but they should be checked on a weekly basis. Canine nail clippers can easily be obtained from pet shops, and many owners find those of the guillotine design easier to use. A nail file can also be used to give a good finish to the nails. However, it is important to

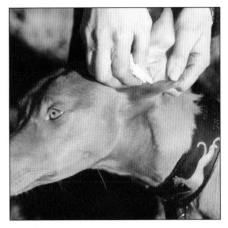

Gently clean the Pharaoh's prominent ears with a soft wipe and ear cleaner. Never enter the ear canal.

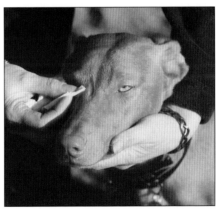

The area around the eyes can be kept clean with soft cotton and a cleansing product made for this purpose, available where you buy pet supplies.

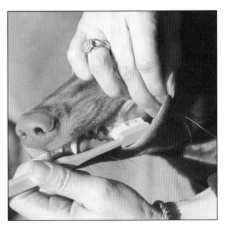

Brushing your Pharaoh Hound's teeth regularly at home is important; this does not have to be an unpleasant task for either of you. Accustom your dog to toothbrushing as a puppy, using products designed for dogs.

Nail Clipping

Quick

Cut Line

Nail Casing

DARK-COLORED NAIL

With black or dark nails, it's best to clip only a small bit of the nail at a time or to use a file where the quick is not visible.

LIGHT-COLORED NAIL

In light-colored nails, clipping is much simpler because you can see the vein (or quick) that grows inside the nail casing.

introduce a Pharaoh to routine nail care from an early age, for many can be very awkward about this.

TEETH
Teeth should always be kept as free from tartar as possible. There are now several canine tooth-cleaning agents available, including the basics, like a toothbrush and canine toothpaste.

TRAVELING WITH YOUR DOG

CAR TRAVEL
You should accustom your Pharaoh Hound to riding in a car at an early age. You may or may not take him in the car often, but at the very least he will need to go to the vet and you do not want these trips to be traumatic for the dog or troublesome for you. The safest way for a dog to ride in the car is in his crate. If he uses a crate in the house, you can use the same crate for travel.

Put the pup in the crate and see how he reacts. If he seems uneasy, you can have a passenger hold him on his lap while you drive. Another option is a specially made safety harness for dogs, which straps the dog in much like a seat belt. Do not let the dog roam loose in the vehicle—this is very dangerous! If you should stop short, your dog can be thrown and injured. If the dog starts climbing on you and pestering you while you are driving, you will not be able to concentrate on the road. It is an unsafe situation for everyone—human and canine.

For long trips, bring along some fresh water and be prepared to stop to let the dog relieve himself. Take with you whatever you need to clean up after him, including some paper towels and perhaps some old rags for use should he have a potty accident in the car or suffer from motion sickness.

AIR TRAVEL

Contact your chosen airline before proceeding with travel plans that include your Pharaoh Hound. The dog will be required to travel in a fiberglass crate and you should always check in advance with the airline regarding specific requirements for the crate's size, type and labeling, as well as any other special travel requirements.

To help put the dog at ease, give him one of his favorite toys in the crate. Do not feed the dog for several hours prior to checking in so that you minimize his need to relieve himself. Some airlines require you to provide documentation as to when the dog was last fed. In any case, a light meal is best. For long trips, you will have to attach food and water bowls to the dog's crate so that airline employees can tend to him between legs of the trip.

PEDICURE TIP

A dog that spends a lot of time outside on a hard surface, such as cement or pavement, will have his nails naturally worn down and may not need to have them trimmed as often, except maybe in the colder months when he is not outside as much. Regardless, it is best to get your dog accustomed to the nail-trimming procedure at an early age so that he is used to it. Some dogs are especially sensitive about having their feet touched, but if a dog has experienced it since puppyhood, it should not bother him.

You can purchase an electric tool to grind down a dog's nails rather than cut them. Some dogs don't seem to mind the electric grinder but will object strongly to nail clippers. See how your dog reacts to his pedicures to help you choose the proper tools.

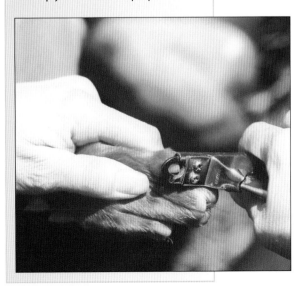

Make sure your dog is properly identified and that your contact information appears on his ID tags and on his crate. Animals travel in a different area of the plane than human passengers, so every rule must be strictly followed so as to prevent the risk of getting separated from your dog.

VACATIONS AND BOARDING

So you want to take a family trip—and you want to include *all* members of the family. You would probably make arrangements for accommodations ahead of time anyway, but this is especially important when traveling with a dog. You do not want to make an overnight stop at the only place around for miles and find out that they do not allow dogs. Also, you do not want to reserve a place for

> **THE FAIR BREED**
> Because Pharaoh Hounds do not have dark pigment, care should be taken when they are outdoors in strong sunshine that their noses and ears do not get burned. Sunblock may be advised for the sun-worshipping Pharaoh.

your family without confirming that you are traveling with a dog because, if it is against their policy, you may not have a place to stay.

Alternatively, if you are traveling and choose not to bring your Pharaoh, you will have to make arrangements for him while you are away. Some options are to take him to a friend's house to stay while you are gone, to have a trusted neighbor stop by often or stay at your house or to bring your dog to a reputable boarding kennel. If you choose to board him at a kennel, you should visit in advance to see the facilities provided, how clean they are and where the dogs are kept. Talk to some of the employees and see how they treat the dogs—do they spend time with the dogs, play with them, exercise them, etc.? Also find out the kennel's policy on vaccinations and what they require. This is for all of the dogs' safety, since when dogs are kept together, there is a greater risk of diseases being passed from dog to dog.

No matter where your travels take you, keep your Pharaoh Hound's safety first in your mind. A sturdy lead and collar, plus ID tags with your contact information, are neccessities.

Ideally, you should select a boarding kennel that is convenient to your home, affordable, clean and professionally run. Make some visits to kennels in your area to meet the staff, see the premises, learn about their services, etc., so you know which facility you will use before you even need it.

IDENTIFICATION

Your Pharaoh is your valued companion and friend. That is why you always keep a close eye on him and you have made sure that he cannot escape from the yard or wriggle out of his collar and run away from you. However, accidents can happen and there may come a time when your dog unexpectedly gets separated from you. If this unfortunate event should occur, the first thing on your mind will be finding him. Proper identification, including an ID tag and possibly a tattoo and/or a microchip, will increase the chances of his being returned to you safely and quickly.

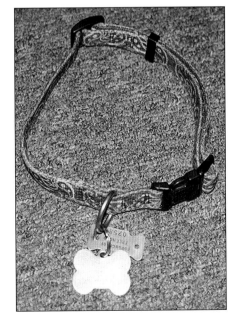

Your Pharaoh Hound must never be without his identification tags, attached securely to his everyday collar.

TRAINING YOUR

PHARAOH HOUND

Left to his own devices, there's no limit to what an inquistive Pharaoh Hound puppy can get into. The owner takes on a challenge in training this unique breed, but the reward is an intelligent, alert, personable and multi-talented canine companion.

Living with an untrained dog is a lot like owning a piano that you do not know how to play—it is a nice object to look at, but it does not do much more than that to bring you pleasure. Now try taking piano lessons, and suddenly the piano comes alive and brings forth magical sounds and rhythms that set your heart singing and your body swaying.

The same is true with your Pharaoh Hound. Any dog is a big responsibility and, if not trained sensibly, may develop unacceptable behavior that annoys you or could even cause family friction.

TRAINING RULES
If you want to be successful in training your dog, you have four rules to obey yourself:
1. Develop an understanding of how a dog thinks.
2. Do not blame the dog for lack of communication.
3. Define your dog's personality and act accordingly.
4. Have patience and be consistent.

To train your Pharaoh Hound, you may like to enroll in an obedience class. Teach him good manners as you learn how and why he behaves the way he does. Find out how to communicate with your dog and how to recognize and understand his communications with you. Suddenly the dog takes on a new role in your life—he is clever, interesting, well-behaved and fun to be with. He demonstrates his bond of devotion to you daily. In other words, your Pharaoh Hound does wonders for your ego because he constantly reminds you that you are not only his leader, you are his hero! Those involved with teaching

dog obedience and counseling owners about their dogs' behavior have discovered some interesting facts about dog ownership. For example, training dogs when they are puppies results in the highest rate of success in developing well-mannered and well-adjusted adult dogs. Training an older dog, from six months to six years of age, can produce almost equal results, providing that the owner accepts the dog's slower rate of learning capability and is willing to work patiently to help the dog succeed at developing to his fullest potential. Unfortunately, many owners of untrained adult dogs lack the patience factor, so they do not persist until their dogs are successful at learning particular behaviors.

Training a puppy aged 10 to 16 weeks (20 weeks at the most) is like working with a dry sponge in a pool of water. The pup soaks up whatever you show him and constantly looks for more things to do and learn. At this early age, his body is not yet producing hormones, and therein lies the reason for such a high rate of success. Without hormones, he is focused on his owners and not particularly interested in investigating other places, dogs, people, etc. You are his leader: his provider of food, water, shelter and security. He latches onto you and wants to

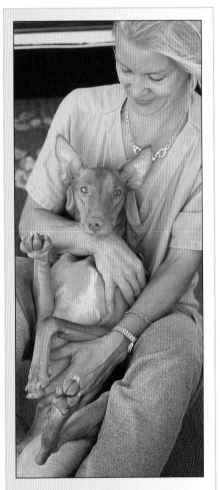

REAP THE REWARDS

If you start with a normal, healthy dog and give him time, patience and some carefully executed lessons, you will reap the rewards of that training for the life of the dog. And what a life it will be! The two of you will find immeasurable pleasure in the companionship you have built together with love, respect and understanding.

stay close. He will usually follow you from room to room, will not let you out of his sight when you are outdoors with him and will respond in like manner to the people and animals you encounter. If you greet a friend warmly, he will be happy to greet the person as well. If, however, you are hesitant or anxious about the approach of a stranger, he will respond accordingly.

Once the puppy begins to produce hormones, his natural curiosity emerges and he begins to investigate the world around

PARENTAL GUIDANCE

Training a dog is a life experience. Many parents admit that much of what they know about raising children they learned from caring for their dogs. Dogs respond to love, fairness and guidance, just as children do. Become a good dog owner and you may become an even better parent.

Training is not just about good behavior, it's about your pup's safety as well. The pup must learn the house rules, including which areas are off-limits.

him. It is at this time when you may notice that the untrained dog begins to wander away from you and even ignore your commands to stay close. When this behavior becomes a problem, the owner has two choices: get rid of the dog or train him. It is strongly urged that you choose the latter option.

There are usually classes within a reasonable distance from your home, but you can also do a lot to train your dog yourself. Sometimes there are classes available but the tuition is too costly. Whatever the circumstances, the solution to training your Pharaoh Hound without formal obedience lessons lies within the pages of this book. This chapter is devoted to helping you train your Pharaoh Hound at home. If the recommended procedures are followed faithfully, you may expect positive results that will prove rewarding both to you and your dog.

Whether your new charge is a puppy or a mature adult, the methods of teaching and the techniques we use in training basic behaviors are the same. After all, no dog, whether puppy or adult, likes harsh or inhumane methods. All creatures, however, respond favorably to gentle motivational methods and sincere praise and encouragement. Now let us get started.

HOUSE-TRAINING

You can train a puppy to relieve himself wherever you choose, but this must be somewhere suitable. You should bear in mind from the outset that when your puppy is old enough to go out in public places, any canine droppings must be removed at once. You will always have to carry with you a small plastic bag or "poop-scoop."

Outdoor training includes such surfaces as grass, soil and

Nothing says "toilet" to a male dog like a big tree where he can leave his calling card.

cement. Indoor training usually means training your dog to newspaper, although this is not usually a viable option with large dogs like Pharaoh Hounds. When deciding on the surface and location that you will want your Pharaoh Hound to use, be sure it is going to be permanent. Training your dog to grass and then changing your mind two months later is extremely difficult for both your dog and you.

MEALTIME

Mealtime should be a peaceful time for your puppy. Do not put his food and water bowls in a high-traffic area in the house. For example, give him his own little corner of the kitchen where he can eat undisturbed and where he will not be underfoot. Do not allow small children or other family members to disturb the pup when he is eating.

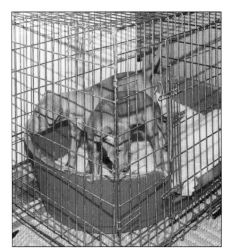

The breeder has accustomed these youngsters to crates before they leave. This gives new owners a head start in crate-training, although once each puppy goes to his new home, he needs a crate all his own.

Next, choose the command you will use each and every time you want your puppy to void. "Hurry up" and "Let's go" are examples of commands commonly used by dog owners. Get in the habit of giving the puppy your chosen relief command before you take him out. That way, when he becomes an adult, you will be able to determine if he wants to go out when you ask him. A confirmation will be signs of interest, such as wagging his tail, watching you intently, going to the door, etc.

Puppy's Needs

Your puppy needs to relieve himself after play periods, after each meal, after he has been sleeping and at any time he indicates that he is looking for a place to urinate or defecate. The urinary and intestinal tract muscles of very young puppies are not fully developed. Therefore, like human babies, puppies need to relieve themselves frequently.

Take your puppy out often—every hour for an eight-week-old, for example, and always immediately after sleeping and eating. The older the puppy, the less often he will need to relieve himself. Finally, as a mature healthy adult, he will require only three to five relief trips per day.

Housing

Since the types of housing and control you provide for your puppy have a direct relationship on the success of house-training, we consider the various aspects of both before we begin training. Taking a new puppy home and turning him loose in your house can be compared to turning a child loose in a sports arena and telling the child that the place is all his! The sheer enormity of the

THINK BEFORE YOU BARK

Dogs are sensitive to their masters' moods and emotions. Use your voice wisely when communicating with your dog. Never raise your voice at your dog unless you are trying to correct him. "Barking" at your dog can become as meaningless as "dogspeak" is to you.

CANINE DEVELOPMENT SCHEDULE

It is important to understand how and at what age a puppy develops into adulthood. If you are a puppy owner, consult the following Canine Development Schedule to determine the stage of development your puppy is currently experiencing. This knowledge will help you as you work with the puppy in the weeks and months ahead.

Period	Age	Characteristics
FIRST TO THIRD	BIRTH TO SEVEN WEEKS	Puppy needs food, sleep and warmth, and responds to simple and gentle touching. Needs mother for security and disciplining. Needs littermates for learning and interacting with other dogs. Pup learns to function within a pack and learns pack order of dominance. Begin socializing pup with adults and children for short periods. Pup begins to become aware of his environment.
FOURTH	EIGHT TO TWELVE WEEKS	Brain is fully developed. Pup needs socializing with outside world. Remove from mother and littermates. Needs to change from canine pack to human pack. Human dominance necessary. Fear period occurs between 8 and 12 weeks. Avoid fright and pain.
FIFTH	THIRTEEN TO SIXTEEN WEEKS	Training and formal obedience should begin. Less association with other dogs, more with people, places, situations. Period will pass easily if you remember this is pup's change-to-adolescence time. Be firm and fair. Flight instinct prominent. Permissiveness and over-disciplining can do permanent damage. Praise for good behavior.
JUVENILE	FOUR TO EIGHT MONTHS	Another fear period about 7 to 8 months of age. It passes quickly, but be cautious of fright and pain. Sexual maturity reached. Dominant traits established. Dog should understand sit, down, come and stay by now.

NOTE: THESE ARE APPROXIMATE TIME FRAMES. ALLOW FOR INDIVIDUAL DIFFERENCES IN PUPPIES.

place would be too much for him to handle.

Instead, offer the puppy clearly defined areas where he can play, sleep, eat and live. A room of the house where the family gathers is the most obvious choice. Puppies are social animals and need to feel a part of the pack right from the start. Hearing your voice, watching you while you are doing things and smelling you nearby are all positive reinforcers that he is now a member of your pack. Usually a family room, the kitchen or a nearby adjoining breakfast area is ideal for providing safety and security for both puppy and owner.

Within that room, there should be a smaller area that the puppy can call his own. An alcove, a wire or fiberglass dog crate or a partitioned-off (not boarded!) corner from which he can view the activities of his new family will be fine. The size of the area or crate is the key factor here. The area must be

> **CALM DOWN**
> Dogs will do anything for your attention. If you reward the dog when he is calm and attentive, you will develop a well-mannered dog. If, on the other hand, you greet your dog excitedly and encourage him to wrestle with you, the dog will greet you the same way and you will have a hyperactive dog on your hands.

large enough for the puppy to lie down and stretch out as well as stand up without rubbing his head on the top, yet small enough so that he cannot relieve himself at one end and sleep at the other without coming into contact with his droppings. Dogs are, by nature, clean animals and will not remain close to their relief areas unless forced to do so. In those cases, they then become dirty dogs and usually remain that way for life.

The designated area should contain clean bedding and a toy. Water must always be available, in a non-spill container, although you'll want to keep an eye on when your pup is drinking so you'll know when he needs "to go."

CONTROL

By *control*, we mean helping the puppy to create a lifestyle pattern that will be compatible to that of his human pack (you).

The predictability of a reliably housebroken dog makes living together clean and easy.

Just as we guide little children to learn our way of life, we must show the puppy when it is time to play, eat, sleep, exercise and even entertain himself.

Your puppy should always sleep in his crate. He should also learn that, during times of household confusion and excessive human activity such as at breakfast when family members are preparing for the day, he can play by himself in relative safety and comfort in his designated area. Each time you leave the puppy alone, he should understand exactly where he is to stay. Puppies are chewers. They cannot tell the difference between lamp cords, television wires, shoes, table legs, etc. Chewing into a television wire, for example, can be fatal to the puppy, while a shorted wire can start a fire in the house.

If the puppy chews on the arm of the chair when he is alone, you will probably discipline him angrily when you get home. Thus, he makes the association that your coming home means he is going to be punished. (He will not remember chewing the chair and is incapable of making the association of the discipline with his naughty deed.) Crating the puppy when you aren't there to supervise prevents his engaging in dangerous and/or destructive behaviors.

LANGUAGE BARRIER

Dogs do not understand our language and have to rely on tone of voice more than just words or sound. They can be trained to react to a certain sound, at a certain volume. If you say "No, Oliver" in a very soft, pleasant voice, it will not have the same meaning as "No, Oliver!!" when you raise your voice.

You should never use the dog's name during a reprimand, just the command "No! " You never want the dog to associate his name with a negative experience or reprimand.

Times of excitement, such as family parties, a friend's visits, etc., can be fun for the puppy, providing he can view the activities from the security of his designated area. He is not underfoot and he is not being fed all sorts of tidbits that will probably cause him stomach distress, yet he still feels a part of the fun.

SCHEDULE

A puppy should be taken to his relief area each time he is released from his designated area, after meals, after play sessions and when he first awakens in the morning (at age eight weeks, this can mean 5 a.m.!). The puppy will indicate that he's ready "to go" by circling or sniffing busily—do not misinterpret these signs. For a

THE SUCCESS METHOD

Success that comes by luck is usually short-lived. Success that comes by well-thought-out proven methods is often more easily achieved and permanent. This is the Success Method. It is designed to give you, the puppy owner, a simple yet proven way to help your puppy develop clean living habits and a feeling of security in his new environment.

6 Steps to Successful Crate Training

1 Tell the puppy "Crate time!" and place him in the crate with a small treat (a piece of cheese or half of a biscuit). Let him stay in the crate for five minutes while you are in the same room. Then release him and praise lavishly. Never release him when he is fussing. Wait until he is quiet before you let him out.

2 Repeat Step 1 several times a day.

3 The next day, place the puppy in the crate as before. Let him stay there for ten minutes. Do this several times.

4 Continue building time in five-minute increments until the puppy stays in his crate for 30 minutes with you in the room. Always take him to his relief area after prolonged periods in his crate.

5 Now go back to Step 1 and let the puppy stay in his crate for five minutes, this time while you are out of the room.

6 Once again, build crate time in five-minute increments with you out of the room. When the puppy will stay willingly in his crate (he may even fall asleep!) for 30 minutes with you out of the room, he will be ready to stay in it for several hours at a time.

HOW MANY TIMES A DAY?

AGE	RELIEF TRIPS
To 14 weeks	10
14–22 weeks	8
22–32 weeks	6
Adulthood	4
(dog stops growing)	

These are estimates, of course, but they are a guide to the *minimum* number of opportunities a dog should have each day to relieve himself.

puppy less than ten weeks of age, a routine of taking him out every hour is necessary. As the puppy grows, he will be able to wait for longer periods of time.

Keep trips to his relief area short. Stay no more than five or six minutes and then return to the house. If he goes during that time, praise him lavishly and take him indoors immediately. If he does not, but he has an accident when you go back indoors, pick him up immediately, say "No! No!" and return to his relief area. Wait a few minutes, then return to the house again. Never hit a puppy or put his face in urine or excrement when he has had an accident!

Once indoors, put the puppy in his crate until you have had time to clean up his accident. Then release him to the family area and watch him more closely than before. Chances are, his accident was a result of your not picking up his signal or waiting too long before offering him the opportunity to relieve himself. Never hold a grudge against the puppy for accidents.

Let the puppy learn that going outdoors means it is time to relieve himself, not play. Once trained, he will be able to play indoors and out and still differentiate between the times for play versus the times for relief.

Help him develop regular hours for naps, being alone, playing by himself and just resting, all in his crate. Encourage him to entertain himself while you are busy with your activities. Let him learn that having you near is comforting, but it is not your main purpose in life to provide him with undivided attention.

Each time you put your puppy in his own area, use the same command, whatever suits best. Soon he will run to his crate or special area when he hears you say those words.

Crate training provides safety for you, the puppy and the

Always clean up after your dog, whether you're in a public place or your own yard.

home. It also provides the puppy with a feeling of security, and that helps the puppy achieve self-confidence and clean habits.

Remember that one of the primary ingredients in house-training your puppy is control. Regardless of your lifestyle, there will always be occasions when you will need to have a place where your dog can stay and be happy and safe. Crate training is the answer for now and in the future.

In conclusion, a few key elements are really all you need for a successful house-training method—consistency, frequency, praise, control and supervision. By following these procedures with a normal, healthy puppy, you and the puppy will soon be past the stage of "accidents" and ready to move on to a clean and rewarding life together.

ROLES OF DISCIPLINE, REWARD AND PUNISHMENT

Discipline, training one to act in accordance with rules, brings order to life. It is as simple as that. Without discipline, particularly in a group society, chaos reigns supreme and the group will eventually perish. Humans and canines are social animals and need some form of discipline in order to function effectively. They must procure food, reproduce to keep the species going and protect their home base and their young.

If there were no discipline in the lives of social animals, they would eventually die from starvation and/or predation by other stronger animals. In the case of domestic canines, dogs need discipline in their lives in order to understand how their pack (you and other family

FEAR AGGRESSION

Pups who are subjected to physical abuse during training commonly end up with behavioral problems as adults. One common result of abuse is fear aggression, in which a dog will lash out, bare his teeth, snarl and finally bite someone by whom he feels threatened. For example, your daughter may be playing with the dog one afternoon. As they play hide-and-seek, she backs the dog into a corner and, as she attempts to tease him playfully, he bites her hand. Examine the cause of this behavior. Did your daughter ever hit the dog? Did someone who resembles your daughter hit or scream at the dog?

Fortunately, fear aggression is relatively easy to correct. Have your daughter engage in only positive activities with the dog, such as feeding, petting and walking. She should not give any corrections or negative feedback. If the dog still growls or cowers away from her, allow someone else to accompany them. After approximately one week, the dog should feel that he can rely on her for many positive things, and he will also be prevented from reacting fearfully towards anyone who might resemble her.

members) functions and how they must act in order to survive.

A large humane society in a highly populated area recently surveyed dog owners regarding their satisfaction with their relationships with their dogs. People who had trained their dogs were 75% more satisfied with their pets than those who had never trained their dogs.

Noted psychologist, Dr. Edward Thorndike established *Thorndike's Theory of Learning*, which states that a behavior that results in a pleasant event tends to be repeated and a behavior that results in an unpleasant event tends not to be repeated. It is this theory on which training methods are based today. For example, if you manipulate a dog to perform a specific behavior and reward him for doing it, he is likely to do it again because he

enjoyed the end result.

Occasionally, punishment, a penalty inflicted for an offense, is necessary. The best type of punishment often comes from an outside source. For example, a child is told not to touch the stove because he may get burned. He disobeys and touches the stove. In doing so, he receives a burn. From that time on, he respects the heat of the stove and avoids contact with it. Therefore, a behavior that results in an unpleasant event tends not to be repeated.

Training a show potential begins in puppyhood. Along with the basic commands, the pup will need to learn to stand and stay for examination by the judge. A treat will keep him focused and standing at attention.

PLAN TO PLAY

The puppy should also have regular play and exercise sessions when he is with you or a family member. Exercise for a very young puppy can consist of a short walk around the house or yard. Playing can include fetching games with a large ball or a special toy. (All puppies teethe and need soft things upon which to chew.) Remember to restrict play periods to indoors within his living area (the family room, for example) until he is completely house-trained.

PRACTICE MAKES PERFECT!

- Have training lessons with your dog every day in several short segments—three to five times a day for a few minutes at a time is ideal.
- Do not have long practice sessions. The dog will become easily bored.
- Never practice when you are tired, ill, worried or in an otherwise negative mood. This will transmit to the dog and may have an adverse effect on his performance.

Think fun, short and above all *positive!* End each session on a high note, rather than a failed exercise, and make sure to give a lot of praise. Enjoy the training and help your dog enjoy it, too.

A good example of a dog's learning the hard way is the dog who chases the house cat. He is told many times to leave the cat alone, yet he persists in teasing the cat. Then, one day he begins chasing the cat but the cat turns and swipes a claw across the dog's face, leaving him with a painful gash on his nose. The final result is that the dog stops chasing the cat.

TRAINING EQUIPMENT

COLLAR AND LEASH

For a Pharaoh Hound, the collar and leash that you use for training must be one with which you are easily able to work, not too heavy for the dog and perfectly safe.

TREATS

Have a bag of treats on hand. Something nutritious and easy to swallow works best. Use a soft treat, a chunk of cheese or a piece of cooked chicken rather than a dry biscuit. By the time the dog has finished chewing a dry treat, he will forget why he is being rewarded in the first place! Using food rewards will not teach a dog to beg at the table—the only way to teach a dog to beg at the table is to give him food from the table. In training, rewarding the dog with a food treat will help him associate praise and the treats with learning new behaviors that obviously please his owner. With the sometimes stubborn Pharaoh Hound, food motivators work wonders.

TRAINING BEGINS: ASK THE DOG A QUESTION

In order to teach your dog anything, you must first get his attention. After all, he cannot learn anything if he is looking away from you with his mind on something else.

To get his attention, ask him "School?" and immediately walk over to him and give him a treat as you tell him "Good dog." Wait a minute or two and repeat the routine, this time with a treat in your hand as you approach within a foot of the dog. Do not go directly to him, but stop about a foot short of him and hold out the treat as you ask "School?" He will see you approaching with a treat in your hand and most likely begin walking toward you. As you meet, give him the treat and praise again.

The third time, ask the question, have a treat in your hand and walk only a short distance toward the dog so that he must walk almost all the way to you. As he reaches you, give him the treat and praise again.

By this time, the dog will

COMMAND STANCE

Stand up straight and authoritatively when giving your dog commands. Do not issue commands when lying on the floor or lying on your back on the sofa. If you are on your hands and knees when you give a command, your dog will think you are positioning yourself to play.

It may help to teach the sit by first guiding the dog into the correct position a few times. Praise him when he assumes a proper sit with your help, and soon he will get the idea and do it on his own.

THE BASIC COMMANDS

TEACHING SIT

Now that you have the dog's attention, attach his leash and hold it in your left hand and a food treat in your right. Place your food hand at the dog's nose and let him lick the treat but not take it from you. Say "Sit" and slowly raise your food hand from in front of the dog's nose up over his head so that he is looking at the ceiling. As he bends his head upward, he will have to bend his knees to maintain his balance. As he bends his knees, he will assume a sit position. At that point, release the food treat and praise lavishly with comments such as "Good dog! Good sit!" Remember to always praise enthusiastically, because dogs relish verbal praise from their

probably be getting the idea that if he pays attention to you, especially when you ask that question, it will pay off in treats and enjoyable activities for him. In other words, he learns that "school" means doing great things with you that are fun and result in positive attention for him.

Remember that the dog does not understand your verbal language; he only recognizes sounds. Your question translates to a series of sounds for him, and those sounds become the signal to go to you and pay attention; if he does, he will get to interact with you plus receive treats and praise.

READY, SIT, GO!
On your marks, get set: train! Most professional trainers agree that the sit command is the place to start your dog's formal education. Sitting is a natural posture for most dogs and they respond to the sit exercise willingly and readily. For every lesson, begin with the sit command, so that you start out on a successful note. Likewise, you should practice the sit command at the end of every lesson as well because you always want to end on a high note.

owners and feel so proud of themselves whenever they accomplish a behavior.

You will not use food forever in getting the dog to obey your commands. Food is only used to teach new behaviors, and once the dog knows what you want when you give a specific command, you will wean him off the food treats but still maintain the verbal praise. After all, you will always have your voice with you, and there will be many times when you have no food rewards but expect the dog to obey.

Teaching Down

Teaching the down exercise is easy when you understand how the dog perceives the down position, and it is very difficult when you do not. Dogs perceive the down, position as a submissive one, therefore, teaching the down exercise using a forceful method can sometimes make the dog develop such a fear of the down that he either runs away when you say "Down" or he attempts to snap at the person who tries to force him down.

Have the dog sit close alongside your left leg, facing in the same direction as you are. Hold the leash in your left hand and a food treat in your right. Now place your left hand lightly on the top of the dog's shoulders where they meet above the

spinal cord. Do not push down on the dog's shoulders; simply rest your left hand there so you can guide the dog to lie down close to your left leg rather than to swing away from your side when he drops.

Now place the food hand at the dog's nose, say "Down" very softly (almost a whisper), and slowly lower the food hand to the dog's front feet. When the food hand reaches the floor,

DOUBLE JEOPARDY

A dog in jeopardy never lies down. He stays alert on his feet because instinct tells him that he may have to run away or fight for his survival. Therefore, if a dog feels threatened or anxious, he will not lie down. Consequently, it is important to keep the dog calm and relaxed as he learns the down exercise.

CONSISTENCY PAYS OFF

Dogs need consistency in their feeding schedule, exercise and relief visits, and in the verbal commands you use. If you use "Stay" on Monday and "Stay here, please" on Tuesday, you will confuse your dog. Don't demand perfect behavior during training sessions and then let him have the run of the house the rest of the day. Above all, lavish praise on your pet consistently every time he does something right. The more he feels he is pleasing you, the more willing he will be to learn.

Distance between handler and dog is gradually increased in the stay exercise. It is best to be in a fenced area or use an extra-long lead, just in case something besides the lesson captures your Pharaoh Hound's interest.

begin moving it forward along the floor in front of the dog. Keep talking softly to the dog, saying things like, "Do you want this treat? You can do this, good dog." Your reassuring tone of voice will help calm the dog as he tries to follow the food hand in order to get the treat.

When the dog's elbows touch the floor, release the food and praise softly. Try to get the dog to maintain that down position for several seconds before you let him sit up again. The goal here is to get the dog to settle down and not feel threatened in the down position.

TEACHING STAY

It is easy to teach the dog to stay in either a sit or a down position. Again, we use food and praise during the teaching process as we help the dog to understand exactly what it is that we are expecting him to do.

To teach the sit/stay, start with the dog sitting on your left side as before and hold the leash in your left hand. Have a food treat in your right hand and place your food hand at the dog's nose. Say "Stay" and step out on your right foot to stand directly in front of the dog, toe to toe, as he licks and nibbles the treat. Be sure to keep his head facing upward to maintain the sit position. Count to five and then swing around to stand next to the dog again with him on your left. As soon as you get back to the original position, release the food and praise lavishly.

To teach the down/stay, do the down as previously described. As soon as the dog lies down, say "Stay" and step out on your right foot just as you

did in the sit/stay. Count to five and then return to stand beside the dog with him on your left side. Release the treat and praise as always.

Within a week or ten days, you can begin to add a bit of distance between you and your dog when you leave him. When you do, use your left hand open with the palm facing the dog as a stay signal, much the same as the hand signal a police officer uses to stop traffic at an intersection. Hold the food treat in your right hand as before, but this time the food is not touching the dog's nose. He will watch the food hand and quickly learn that he is going to get that treat as soon as you return to his side.

When you can stand 3 feet away from your dog for 30 seconds, you can then begin building time and distance in both stays. Eventually, the dog can be expected to remain in the stay position for prolonged periods of time until you return to him or call him to you. Always praise lavishly when he stays.

"WHERE ARE YOU?"

When calling the dog, do not say "Come." Say things like, "Rover, where are you? See if you can find me! I have a biscuit for you!" Keep up a constant line of chatter with coaxing sounds and frequent questions such as "Where are you?" The dog will learn to follow the sound of your voice to locate you and receive his reward.

TEACHING COME

If you make teaching "come" a fun experience, you should never have a student that does not love the game or that fails to come when called. The secret, it seems, is never to teach the word "come." At times when an owner most wants his dog to come when called, the owner is likely to be upset or anxious and he allows these feelings to come through in the tone of his voice when he calls his dog. Hearing that desperation in his owner's voice, the dog fears the results of going to him and therefore either disobeys outright or runs in the opposite direction. The secret, therefore, is to teach the dog a

Don't make training sessions all work! Your Pharaoh Hound will jump for joy at a chance for fun time with his favorite playmate...you!

playing the game and that each person has a big celebration awaiting his success at locating them. Once he learns to love the game, simply calling out "Where are you?" will bring him running from wherever he is when he hears that all-important question.

The come command is recognized as one of the most important things to teach a dog, but there are trainers who work with thousands of dogs and never teach the actual word "come." Yet these dogs will race to respond to a person who uses the dog's name followed by "Where are you?" For example, a woman has a 12-year-old companion dog who went blind, but who never fails to locate her owner when asked, "Where are you?'

Children, in particular, love to play this game with their dogs. Children can hide in smaller places like a bathtub, behind a bed or under a table. The dog needs to work a little bit

game and, when you want him to come to you, simply play the game. It is practically a no-fail solution!

To begin, have several members of your family take a few food treats and each go into a different room in the house. Take turns calling the dog, and each person should celebrate the dog's finding him with a treat and lots of happy praise. When a person calls the dog, he is actually inviting the dog to find him and get a treat as a reward for "winning."

A few turns of the "Where are you?" game and the dog will understand that everyone is

"COME" ... BACK

Never call your dog to come to you for a correction or scold him when he reaches you. That is the quickest way to turn a come command into "Go away fast!" Dogs think only in the present tense, and your dog will connect the scolding with coming to you, not with the misbehavior of a few moments earlier.

harder to find these hiding places, but, when he does, he loves to celebrate with a treat and a tussle with a favorite youngster.

TEACHING HEEL

Heeling means that the dog walks beside the owner without pulling. It takes time and patience on the owner's part to succeed at teaching the dog that he (the owner) will not proceed unless the dog is walking calmly beside him. Pulling out ahead on the leash is definitely not accept-able behavior.

Begin by holding the leash in your left hand as the dog sits beside your left leg. Move the loop end of the leash to your right hand but keep your left hand short on the leash so it keeps the dog in close next to you. Say "Heel" and step forward on your left foot. Keep the dog close to you and take three steps. Stop and have the dog sit next to you in what we now call the heel position. Praise verbally, but do not touch the dog. Hesitate a moment and begin again with "Heel," taking three steps and stopping, at which point the dog is told to sit again.

Your goal here is to have the dog walk those three steps without pulling on the leash. Once he will walk calmly beside you for three steps without

pulling, increase the number of steps you take to five. When he will walk politely beside you while you take five steps, you can increase the length of your walk to ten steps. Keep increasing the length of your stroll until the dog will walk quietly beside you without pulling as long as you want him to heel. When you stop heeling, indicate to the dog that the

TUG OF WALK?
If you begin teaching the heel by allowing the pup to tug on the lead and pull you along, he misinterprets this action as an acceptable form of taking a walk. When you pull back on the leash to counteract his pulling, he reads that tug as a signal to pull even harder!

two of you are not going anywhere until he is beside you and moving at your pace, not his. It may take some time just standing there to convince the dog that you are the leader and you will be the one to decide on the direction and speed of your travel.

Each time the dog looks up at you or slows down to give a slack leash between the two of you, quietly praise him and say, "Good heel. Good dog." Eventually, the dog will begin to respond and within a few days he will be walking politely beside you without pulling on the leash. At first, the training sessions should be kept short and very positive; soon the dog will be able to walk nicely with you for increasingly longer distances. Remember also to give the dog free time and the opportunity to run and play when you have finished heel practice.

HEELING WELL
Teach your dog to heel in an enclosed area. Once you think the dog will obey reliably and you want to attempt advanced obedience exercises such as off-lead heeling, test him in a fenced-in area so he cannot run away.

WEANING OFF FOOD IN TRAINING

Food is used in training new behaviors. Once the dog understands what behavior goes with a specific command, it is time to start weaning him off the food treats. At first, give a treat after each exercise. Then, start to give a treat only after every other exercise. Mix up the times when you offer a food reward and the

exercise is over by verbally praising as you pet him and say "OK, good dog." The "OK" is used as a release word, meaning that the exercise is finished and the dog is free to relax.

If you are dealing with a dog who insists on pulling you around, simply "put on your brakes" and stand your ground until the dog realizes that the

> **TRAINING TIP**
>
> If you are walking your dog and he suddenly stops and looks straight into your eyes, ignore him. Pull the leash and lead him into the direction you want to walk.

times when you only offer praise so that the dog will never know when he is going to receive both food and praise and when he is going to receive only praise. This is called a variable-ratio reward system and it proves successful because there is always the chance that the owner will produce a treat, so the dog never stops trying for that reward. No matter what, *always* give verbal praise.

OBEDIENCE CLASSES

It is a good idea to enroll in an obedience class if one is available in your area. If yours is a show dog, handling classes would be more appropriate. Many areas have dog clubs that offer basic obedience training as well as preparatory classes for obedience competition. There are also local dog trainers who offer similar classes.

At obedience trials, dogs can earn titles at various levels of competition. The beginning levels of competition include basic behaviors such as sit, down, heel, etc. The more

advanced levels of competition include jumping, retrieving, scent discrimination and signal work. The advanced levels require a dog and owner to put a lot of time effort and patience into their training, and the titles that can be earned at these levels of competition are very prestigious.

OTHER ACTIVITIES FOR LIFE

Whether a dog is trained in the structured environment of a class or alone with his owner at home, there are many activities that can bring fun and rewards to both owner and dog once they have mastered basic control.

The time you invest in training a show dog will pay off as your Pharaoh Hound stands beautifully in the ring, her attention on you and looking her regal best.

HOW TO WEAN THE "TREAT HOG"

If you have trained your dog by rewarding him with a treat each time he performs a command, he may soon decide that without the treat, he won't sit, stay or come. The best way to fix this problem is to start asking your dog to do certain commands twice before being rewarded. Slowly increase the number of commands given and then vary the number: three sits and a treat one day, five sits for a biscuit the next day, etc. Your dog will soon realize that there is no set number of sits before he gets his reward and he'll likely do it the first time you ask in the hope of being rewarded sooner rather than later.

Teaching the dog to help out around the home, in the yard or on the farm provides great satisfaction to both dog and owner. In addition, the dog's help makes life a little easier for his owner and raises his stature as a valued companion to his family. It helps give the dog a purpose by occupying his mind and providing an outlet for his energy.

Backpacking is an exciting and healthy activity that the dog can be taught without assistance from more than his owner. The exercise of walking and climbing is good for man and dog alike, and the bond that they develop together is priceless. The rule of thumb for backpacking is never to let the dog carry more than one-sixth of his body weight.

If you are interested in participating in organized competition with your Pharaoh Hound, there are activities other than obedience in which you and your dog can become involved. Lure coursing, of course, is the most rewarding event for Pharaoh Hounds, and the AKC offers trials that will challenge and excite owners and dogs alike. Agility is a popular sport where dogs run through an obstacle course that includes various jumps, tunnels and other exercises to test the dog's speed and coordination. The owners run beside their dogs to give commands and to guide them through the course. Although competitive, the focus is on fun—it's fun to do, fun to watch and great exercise.

Training for an agility jump. The jump is set at a low height and a treat is used to get the dog to the other side. The Pharaoh is a natural jumper and athlete, so these exercises are easy and enjoyable for the dog.

"I got it!" Training for lure coursing with rags tied to the end of a long string will entice the dog to chase and catch his "quarry."

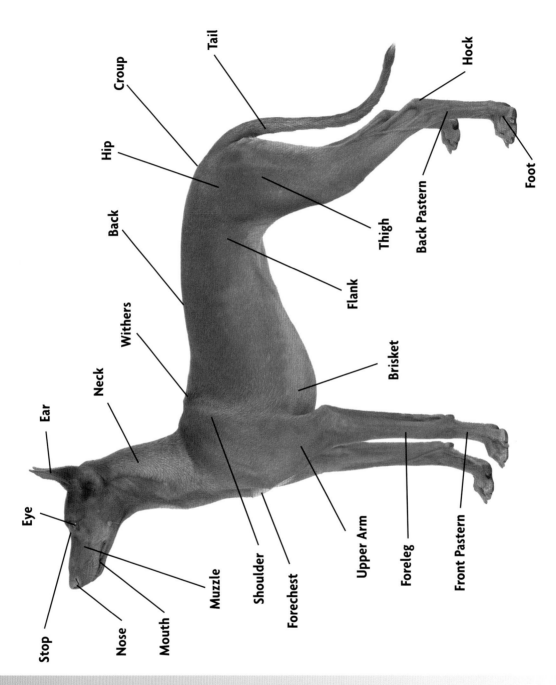

Tail

Croup

Hock

Hip

Thigh

Back

Back Pastern

Foot

Withers

Flank

Neck

Brisket

Ear

Eye

Upper Arm

Stop

Muzzle

Foreleg

Nose

Shoulder

Mouth

Forechest

Front Pastern

Physical Structure of the Pharaoh Hound

PHARAOH HOUND

Dogs suffer from many of the same physical illnesses as people. They might even share many of the same psychological problems. Since people usually know more about human diseases than canine maladies, many of the terms used in this chapter will be familiar but not necessarily those used by veterinarians. We will use the term *x-ray*, instead of the more acceptable term *radiograph*. We will also use the familiar term *symptoms* even though dogs don't have symptoms, which are verbal descriptions of the patient's feelings; dogs have *clinical signs*. Since dogs can't speak, we have to look for clinical signs...but we still use the term *symptoms* in this book.

As a general rule, medicine is *practiced*. That term is not arbitrary. Medicine is a constantly changing art as we learn more and more about genetics, electronic aids (like CAT scans and MRIs) and daily laboratory advances. There are many dog maladies, like canine hip dysplasia, which are not universally treated in the same manner. For example, some vets opt for surgical treaments more often than others do.

SELECTING A QUALIFIED VET
Your selection of a veterinarian should be based upon personality and skills with dogs as well as his convenience to your home. You want a vet who is close because you might have emergencies or need to make multiple visits for treatments. You want a vet who has services that you might require such as a boarding kennel and tattooing, and of course a good reputation for ability and responsiveness. There is nothing more frustrating than having to wait a day or more to get a response from your vet.

All vets are licensed and their diplomas and/or certificates should be displayed in their waiting rooms. Your vet should be capable of dealing with maintaining your dog's health, as well as infections, injuries, routine surgeries and the like. There are, however, many veterinary specialties that usually require further studies and internships. These include specialists in heart problems (veterinary cardiologists), skin problems (veterinary dermatologists), teeth and gum problems (veterinary dentists), eye problems (veterinary

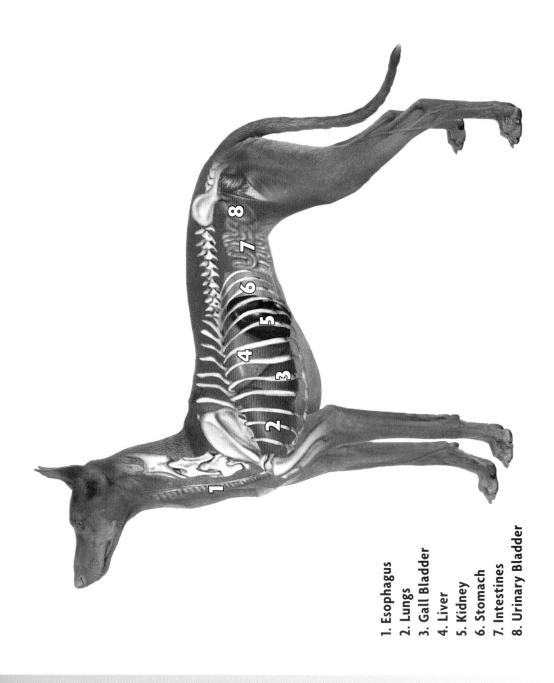

1. Esophagus
2. Lungs
3. Gall Bladder
4. Liver
5. Kidney
6. Stomach
7. Intestines
8. Urinary Bladder

Internal Organs of the Pharaoh Hound

ophthalmologists) and x-rays (veterinary radiologists), as well as vets who have specialties in bones, muscles or certain organs.

When the problem affecting your dog is serious, it is not unusual or impudent to get another medical opinion, although it is wise and courteous to advise the veterinarians concerned about this. You might also want to compare costs among several veterinarians. Sophisticated health care and veterinary services can be very costly. It is not infrequent that important decisions about which treatment route to take are based upon financial considerations.

PREVENTATIVE MEDICINE

It is much easier, less costly and more effective to practice preventative medicine than to fight bouts of illness and disease. Properly bred puppies come from parents who were selected based upon their genetic-disease profiles. Their dam should have been vaccinated, free of all internal and external parasites and properly nourished. For these reasons, a visit to the vet who cared for the dam is recommended. The dam can pass on disease resistance to her puppies, which can last for eight to ten weeks. She can also pass on parasites and many infections. That's why you should learn as much about the dam's health as possible.

Breakdown of Veterinary Income by Category

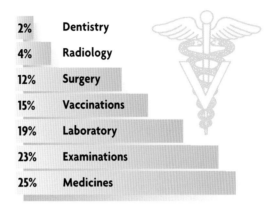

%	Category
2%	Dentistry
4%	Radiology
12%	Surgery
15%	Vaccinations
19%	Laboratory
23%	Examinations
25%	Medicines

A typical vet's income, categorized according to services performed. This survey dealt with small-animal (pets) practices.

WEANING TO BRINGING PUPPY HOME Puppies should be weaned by the time they are about two months old. A puppy that remains for at least eight weeks with his dam and littermates usually adapts better to other dogs and people later in life.

Some new owners have their puppy examined by a vet immediately, which is a good idea. Unless the pup is overtired by the journey home. In that case, an appointment should be arranged for the next day.

The puppy will have his teeth examined and have his skeletal conformation and general health checked prior to certification by the vet. Pharaoh puppies can have problems with their kneecaps and undescended testicles; other common puppy problems include cataracts and other eye problems and heart murmurs. Your vet

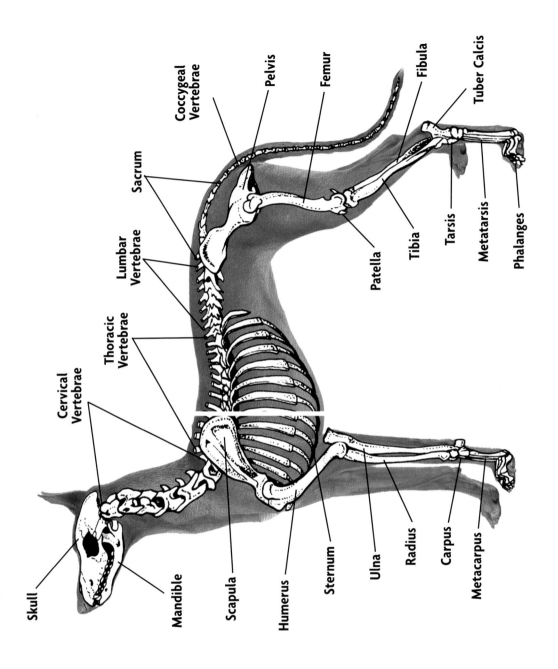

Coccygeal Vertebrae

Pelvis

Femur

Fibula

Tuber Calcis

Sacrum

Lumbar Vertebrae

Tibia

Patella

Tarsis

Metatarsis

Phalanges

Thoracic Vertebrae

Cervical Vertebrae

Skull

Mandible

Scapula

Humerus

Sternum

Ulna

Radius

Carpus

Metacarpus

Skeletal Structure of the Pharaoh Hound

might also have training in temperament evaluation. At the first visit, your vet will set up your pup's vaccination schedule.

VACCINATION SCHEDULING

Most vaccinations are given by injection and should only be done by a vet. From the onset of your relationship with your vet, be sure to advise him that Pharaoh Hounds can be particularly sensitive to inoculations and other injections. Both he and you should keep a record of the date of the injection, the identification of the vaccine and the amount given. Some vets give a first vaccination at six weeks, but most dog breeders prefer the course not to commence until about eight weeks because of negating any antibodies passed on by the dam. The vaccination scheduling is usually based on a two- to four-week cycle. You must take your vet's advice regarding when to vaccinate as this may differ according to the vaccine used.

Most vaccinations immunize your puppy against viruses. The usual vaccines contain immunizing doses of several different viruses such as distemper, parvovirus, parainfluenza and hepatitis, although

HEALTH AND VACCINATION SCHEDULE

AGE IN WEEKS:	6TH	8TH	10TH	12TH	14TH	16TH	20-24TH	52ND
Worm Control	✔	✔	✔	✔	✔	✔	✔	
Neutering							✔	
Heartworm		✔		✔		✔	✔	
Parvovirus	✔		✔		✔		✔	✔
Distemper		✔		✔		✔		✔
Hepatitis		✔		✔		✔		✔
Leptospirosis								✔
Parainfluenza	✔		✔		✔			✔
Dental Examination		✔					✔	✔
Complete Physical		✔					✔	✔
Coronavirus				✔			✔	✔
Canine Cough	✔							
Hip Dysplasia							✔	
Rabies							✔	

Vaccinations are not instantly effective. It takes about two weeks for the dog's immune system to develop antibodies. Most vaccinations require annual booster shots. Your vet should guide you in this regard.

The normal, healthy hairs of a typical dog, enlarged about 200 times normal size. The inset shows the tip of a fine, growing hair, magnified about 2,000 times normal size.

some vets recommend separate vaccines for each disease. There are other vaccines available when the puppy is at risk. You should rely upon professional advice. This is especially true for the booster-shot program. Most vaccination programs require a booster when the puppy is a year old and once a year thereafter. In some cases, circumstances may require more or less frequent immunizations. Canine cough, more formally known as tracheo-bronchitis, is treated with a vaccine that is sprayed into the dog's nostrils. Canine cough is usually included in routine vaccination, but this is often not so effective as for other major diseases.

FIVE TO TWELVE MONTHS OF AGE

Unless you intend to breed or show your dog, neutering the puppy at six months of age is recommended. Discuss this with your vet. Neutering/spaying has proven to be extremely beneficial to both male and female dogs. Besides eliminating the possibility of pregnancy and

DISEASE REFERENCE CHART

	What is it?	What causes it?	Symptoms
Leptospirosis	Severe disease that affects the internal organs; can be spread to people.	A bacterium, which is often carried by rodents, that enters through mucous membranes and spreads quickly throughout the body.	Range from fever, vomiting and loss of appetite in less severe cases to shock, irreversible kidney damage and possibly death in most severe cases.
Rabies	Potentially deadly virus that infects warm-blooded mammals.	Bite from a carrier of the virus, mainly wild animals.	1st stage: dog exhibits change in behavior, fear. 2nd stage: dog's behavior becomes more aggressive. 3rd stage: loss of coordination, trouble with bodily functions.
Parvovirus	Highly contagious virus, potentially deadly.	Ingestion of the virus, which is usually spread through the feces of infected dogs.	Most common: severe diarrhea. Also vomiting, fatigue, lack of appetite.
Canine cough	Contagious respiratory infection.	Combination of types of bacteria and virus. Most common: *Bordetella bronchiseptica* bacteria and parainfluenza virus.	Chronic cough.
Distemper	Disease primarily affecting respiratory and nervous system.	Virus that is related to the human measles virus.	Mild symptoms such as fever, lack of appetite and mucus secretion progress to evidence of brain damage, "hard pad."
Hepatitis	Virus primarily affecting the liver.	Canine adenovirus type I (CAV-1). Enters system when dog breathes in particles.	Lesser symptoms include listlessness, diarrhea, vomiting. More severe symptoms include "blue-eye" (clumps of virus in eye).
Coronavirus	Virus resulting in digestive problems.	Virus is spread through infected dog's feces.	Stomach upset evidenced by lack of appetite, vomiting, diarrhea.

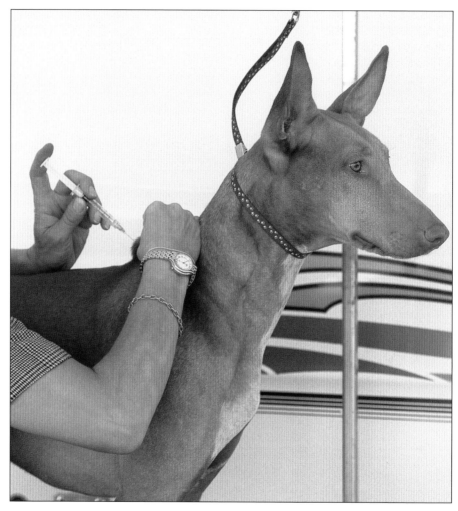

Your vet will start your Pharaoh Hound's vaccination program when the dog is young and will manage his booster inoculations throughout the dog's life.

pyometra in bitches and testicular cancer in males, it greatly reduces the risk of breast cancer in bitches and prostate cancer in male dogs.

Your vet should provide your puppy with a thorough dental evaluation at six months of age, ascertaining whether all of the permanent teeth have erupted properly. A home dental-care regimen should be initiated at six months, including brushing weekly and providing good dental devices (such as nylon bones). Regular dental care promotes healthy teeth, fresh breath and a longer life.

OLDER THAN ONE YEAR

Once a year, your full-grown dog should visit the vet for an examination and vaccination boosters, if needed. Some vets recommend blood tests, thyroid level check and dental evaluation to accompany these annual visits. A thorough clinical evaluation by the vet can provide critical background information for your dog. Blood tests are often performed at one year of age, and dental examinations should be part of routine check-ups. In the long run, quality preventative care for your pet can save money, teeth and lives.

SKIN PROBLEMS IN PHARAOH HOUNDS

Vets are consulted by dog owners for skin problems more than for any other group of diseases or maladies. Dogs' skin is almost as sensitive as human skin and both can suffer from almost the same ailments (though the occurrence of acne in most dogs is rare). For this reason, veterinary derma-tology has developed into a specialty practiced by many veterinarians.

Since many skin problems have visual symptoms that are almost identical, it requires the skill of an experienced veterinary dermatologist to identify and cure many of the more severe skin disorders. Pet shops sell many treatments for skin problems, but most of the treatments are directed at symptoms and not the underlying problem(s). If your dog is suffering from a skin disorder, you should seek professional assistance as quickly as possible. As with all diseases, the earlier a problem is identified and treated, the more likely is a complete cure.

HEREDITARY SKIN DISORDERS

Veterinary dermatologists are currently researching a number of skin disorders that are believed to have hereditary bases. These inherited diseases are transmitted by both parents, who appear (phenotypically) normal but have a recessive gene for the disease, meaning that they carry, but are not affected by, the disease. These diseases pose serious problems to breeders because in some instances there is no method of identifying carriers. Often the secondary diseases associated with these skin conditions are even more debilitating than the disorder itself, including cancers and respiratory problems.

Among the hereditary skin disorders, for which the mode of inheritance is known, are: acrodermatitis, cutaneous asthenia (Ehlers-Danlos syndrome), sebaceous adenitis, cyclic hematopoiesis, dermatomyositis, IgA deficiency, color dilution alopecia and nodular dermatofi-brosis. Some of these disorders are limited to one or two breeds and others affect a large number of breeds. All inherited diseases must be diagnosed and treated by a veterinary specialist.

PARASITE BITES

Many of us are allergic to insect bites. The bites itch, erupt and may even become infected. Dogs have the same reaction to fleas, ticks and/or mites. When an insect lands on you, you have the chance to whisk it away with your hand. Unfortunately, when your dog is bitten by a flea, tick or mite, he can only scratch it away or bite it. By the time the dog has been bitten, the parasite has done some of its damage. It may also have laid eggs to cause further problems in the near future. The itching from parasite bites is probably due to the saliva injected into the site when the parasite sucks the dog's blood.

AUTO-IMMUNE SKIN CONDITIONS

Auto-immune skin conditions are commonly referred to as being allergic to yourself, while allergies are usually inflammatory reactions to an outside stimulus. Auto-immune diseases cause serious damage to the tissues that are involved.

The best known auto-immune disease is lupus, which affects people as well as dogs. The symptoms are variable and may affect the kidneys, bones, blood chemistry and skin. It can be fatal to both dogs and humans, though it is not thought to be transmissible. It is usually successfully treated with cortisone, prednisone or a similar corticosteroid, but extensive use of these drugs can have harmful side effects.

ACRAL LICK GRANULOMA

Many large dogs have a very poorly understood syndrome called acral lick granuloma. The manifestation of the problem is the dog's tireless attack at a specific area of the body, almost always the legs or paws. The dog licks so intensively that he removes the hair and skin, leaving an ugly, large wound. Tiny protuberances, which are outgrowths of new capillaries, bead on the surface of the wound. Owners who notice their dogs' biting and chewing at their extremities should have the vet determine the cause. If lick granuloma is identified, although there is no absolute cure, corticosteroids are the most common treatment.

AIRBORNE ALLERGIES

Just as humans have hay fever, rose fever and other fevers from which they suffer during the pollinating season, many dogs suffer from the same allergies. When the pollen count is high, your dog might suffer, but don't expect him to sneeze and have a runny nose. Dogs react to pollen allergies the same way they react to fleas—they scratch and bite themselves.

Dogs, like humans, can be tested for allergens. Discuss the testing with your veterinary dermatologist.

FOOD PROBLEMS

FOOD ALLERGIES

Dogs can be allergic to many foods that are best-sellers and highly recommended by breeders and vets. Changing the brand of food that you buy may not eliminate the problem if the element to which the dog is allergic is contained in the new brand.

Recognizing a food allergy is difficult. Humans vomit or have rashes when we eat a food to which we are allergic. Dogs neither vomit nor (usually) develop a rash. They react in the same manner as they do to an airborne or flea allergy; they itch, scratch and bite, thus making the diagnosis extremely difficult. While pollen allergies and parasite bites are usually seasonal, food allergies are year-round problems.

FOOD INTOLERANCE

Food intolerance is the inability of the dog to completely digest certain foods. For example, puppies that may have done very well on their mother's milk may

HOW TO PREVENT BLOAT
Research has confirmed that the structure of deep-chested breeds contributes to their predisposition to bloat. Nevertheless, there are several precautions that you can take to reduce the risk of this condition:
• Feed your dog twice daily rather than offer one big meal.
• Do not exercise your dog for at least one hour before and two hours after he has eaten.
• Make certain that your dog is calm and not overly excited while he is eating. It has been proven that nervous or overly excited dogs are more prone to develop bloat.
• Add a small portion of moist meat product to his dry food ration.
• Serve his meals and water in an elevated bowl stand, which avoids the dog's craning his neck while eating and drinking.
• To prevent your dog from gobbling his food too quickly, and thereby swallowing air, put some large (unswallowable) toys into his bowl so that he will have to eat around them to get his food.
• Never allow him to gulp water, and limit water intake at meals.

not do well on cow's milk. The result of this food intolerance may be loose bowels, passing gas and stomach pains. These are the only obvious symptoms of food intolerance and that makes diagnosis difficult.

TREATING FOOD PROBLEMS

It is possible to handle food allergies and food intolerance yourself. Put your dog on a diet that he has never had. Obviously, if he has never eaten this new food, he can't have been allergic or intolerant of it. Start with a single ingredient that is not in the dog's diet at the present time. Ingredients like chopped beef or chicken are common in dogs' diets, so try something more exotic like fish, lamb or some other quality source of protein. Keep the dog on this diet (with no additives) for a month. If the symptoms of food allergy or intolerance disappear, chances are your dog has a food allergy.

Don't think that the single ingredient cured the problem. You still must find a suitable diet and ascertain which ingredient in the original diet was objectionable. This is most easily done by adding ingredients to the new diet one at a time. Let the dog stay on the modified diet for a month before you add another ingredient. Eventually, you will determine the ingredient that caused the adverse reaction.

An alternative method is to carefully study the ingredients in the diet to which your dog is allergic or intolerant. Identify the main ingredient in this diet and eliminate the main ingredient by buying a different food that does not have that ingredient. Keep experimenting until the symptoms disappear after one month on the new diet.

DETECTING BLOAT

As important as it is to take precautions against bloat/gastric torsion, it is of equal importance to recognize the symptoms. It is necessary for your Pharaoh Hound to get immediate veterinary attention if you notice any of the following signs:

- Your dog's stomach starts to distend, ending up large and as tight as a football;
- Your dog is dribbling, as no saliva can be swallowed;
- Your dog makes frequent attempts to vomit but cannot bring anything up due to the stomach's being closed off;
- Your dog is distressed from pain;
- Your dog starts to suffer from clinical shock, meaning that there is not enough blood in the dog's circulation as the hard, dilated stomach stops the blood from returning to the heart to be pumped around the body. Clinical shock is indicated by pale gums and tongue, as they have been starved of blood. The shocked dog also has glazed, staring eyes.

You have minutes—yes, *minutes*—to get your dog into surgery. If you see any of these symptoms at any time of the day or night, get to the vet immediately. Someone will have to phone and warn that you are on your way (which is a justification for the invention of the cellular phone!), so that they can be prepared to get your pet on the operating table.

First Aid at a Glance

Burns
Place the affected area under cool water;
use ice if only a small area is burnt.

Bee stings/Insect bites
Apply ice to relieve swelling;
antihistamine dosed properly.

Animal bites
Clean any bleeding area; apply pressure
until bleeding subsides; go to the vet.

Spider bites
Use cold compress and a pressurized
pack to inhibit venom's spreading.

Antifreeze poisoning
Induce vomiting with hydrogen peroxide.
Seek *immediate* veterinary help!

Fish hooks
Removal best handled by vet;
hook must be cut in order to remove.

Snake bites
Pack ice around bite; contact vet
quickly; identify snake for proper
antivenin.

Car accident
Move dog from roadway with blanket;
seek veterinary aid.

Shock
Calm the dog; keep him warm; seek
immediate veterinary help.

Nosebleed
Apply cold compress to the nose; apply
pressure to any visible abrasion.

Bleeding
Apply pressure above the area; treat
wound by applying a cotton pack.

Heat stroke
Submerge dog in cold bath; cool down
with fresh air and water; go to the vet.

Frostbite/Hypothermia
Warm the dog with a warm bath, electric
blankets or hot water bottles.

Abrasions
Clean the wound and wash out
thoroughly with fresh water;
apply antiseptic.

 *Remember: an injured dog may attempt
to bite a helping hand from fear and confusion.
Always muzzle the dog before trying to offer assistance.*

Number-One Killer Disease in Dogs: CANCER

In every age, there is a word associated with a disease or plague that causes humans to shudder. In the 21st century, that word is "cancer." Just as cancer is the leading cause of death in humans, it claims nearly half the lives of dogs that die from a natural disease as well as half the dogs that die over the age of ten years.

Described as a genetic disease, cancer becomes a greater risk as the dog ages. Vets and dog owners have become increasingly aware of the threat of cancer to dogs. Statistics reveal that one dog in every five will develop cancer, the most common of which is skin cancer. Many cancers, including prostate, ovarian and breast cancer, can be avoided by spaying and neutering our dogs by the age of six months.

Early detection of cancer can save or extend a dog's life, so it is absolutely vital for owners to have their dogs examined by a qualified vet or oncologist immediately upon detection of any abnormality. Certain dietary guidelines have also proven to reduce the onset and spread of cancer. Foods based on fish rather than beef, due to the presence of Omega-3 fatty acids, are recommended. Other amino acids such as glutamine have significant benefits for canines, particularly those breeds that show a greater susceptibility to cancer.

Cancer management and treatments promise hope for future generations of canines. Since the disease is genetic, breeders should never breed a dog whose parents, grandparents and any related siblings have developed cancer. It is difficult to know whether to exclude an otherwise healthy dog from a breeding program, as the disease does not manifest itself until the dog's senior years.

RECOGNIZE CANCER WARNING SIGNS

Since early detection can possibly rescue your dog from becoming a cancer statistic, it is essential for owners to recognize the possible signs and seek the assistance of a qualified professional.

- Abnormal bumps or lumps that continue to grow
- Bleeding or discharge from any body cavity
- Persistent stiffness or lameness
- Recurrent sores or sores that do not heal
- Inappetence
- Breathing difficulties
- Weight loss
- Bad breath or odors
- General malaise and fatigue
- Eating and swallowing problems
- Difficulty urinating and defecating

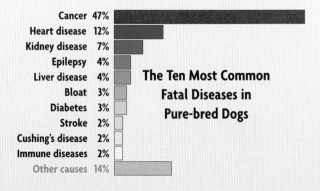

Disease	%
Cancer	47%
Heart disease	12%
Kidney disease	7%
Epilepsy	4%
Liver disease	4%
Bloat	3%
Diabetes	3%
Stroke	2%
Cushing's disease	2%
Immune diseases	2%
Other causes	14%

The Ten Most Common Fatal Diseases in Pure-bred Dogs

CDS: COGNITIVE DYSFUNCTION SYNDROME
"Old-Dog Syndrome"

There are many ways for you to evaluate old-dog syndrome. Veterinarians have defined CDS (cognitive dysfunction syndrome) as the gradual deterioration of cognitive abilities. These are indicated by changes in the dog's behavior. When a dog changes his routine response, and maladies have been eliminated as the cause of these behavioral changes, then CDS is the usual diagnosis.

More than half the dogs over eight years old suffer from some form of CDS. The older the dog, the more chance he has of suffering from CDS. In humans, doctors often dismiss the CDS behavioral changes as part of "winding down."

There are four major signs of CDS: frequent potty accidents inside the home, sleeping much more or much less than normal, acting confused and failing to respond to social stimuli.

SYMPTOMS OF CDS

FREQUENT POTTY ACCIDENTS
- *Urinates in the house.*
- *Defecates in the house.*
- *Doesn't signal that he wants to go out.*

SLEEP PATTERNS
- *Awakens more slowly.*
- *Sleeps more than normal during the day.*
- *Sleeps less during the night.*

CONFUSION
- *Goes outside and just stands there.*
- *Appears confused with a faraway look in his eyes.*
- *Hides more often.*
- *Doesn't recognize friends.*
- *Doesn't come when called.*
- *Walks around listlessly and without a destination.*

FAILURE TO RESPOND TO SOCIAL STIMULI
- *Comes to people less frequently, whether called or not.*
- *Doesn't tolerate petting for more than a short time.*
- *Doesn't come to the door when you return home.*

A male dog flea, *Ctenocephalides canis.*

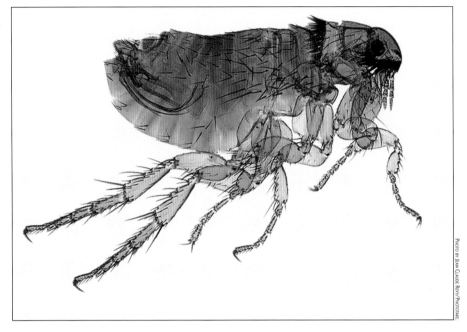

PHOTO BY JEAN CLAUDE REVY/PHOTOTAKE

EXTERNAL PARASITES

FLEAS

Of all the problems to which dogs are prone, none is more well known and frustrating than fleas. Flea infestation is relatively simple to cure but difficult to prevent. Parasites that are harbored inside the body are a bit more difficult to eradicate but they are easier to control.

To control flea infestation, you have to understand the flea's life cycle. Fleas are often thought of as a summertime problem, but centrally heated homes have changed the patterns and fleas can be found at any time of the year. The most effective method of flea control is a two-stage approach: one stage to kill the adult fleas, and the other to control the development of pre-adult fleas. Unfortunately, no single active ingredient is effective against all stages of the life cycle.

FLEA KILLER CAUTION— "POISON"

Flea-killers are poisonous. You should not spray these toxic chemicals on areas of a dog's body that he licks, including his genitals and his face. Flea killers taken internally are a better answer, but check with your vet in case internal therapy is not advised for your dog.

LIFE CYCLE STAGES

During its life, a flea will pass through four life stages: egg, larva, pupa or nymph and adult. The adult stage is the most visible and irritating stage of the flea life cycle, and this is why the majority of flea-control products concentrate on this stage. The fact is that adult fleas account for only 1% of the total flea population, and the other 99% exist in pre-adult stages, i.e., eggs, larvae and nymphs. The pre-adult stages are barely visible to the naked eye.

THE LIFE CYCLE OF THE FLEA

Eggs are laid on the dog, usually in quantities of about 20 or 30, several times a day. The adult female flea must have a blood meal before each egg-laying session. When first laid, the eggs will cling to the dog's hair, as the eggs are still moist. However, they will quickly dry out and fall from the dog, especially if the dog moves around or scratches. Many eggs will fall off in the dog's favorite area or an area in which he spends a lot of time, such as his bed.

Once the eggs fall from the dog onto the carpet or furniture, they will hatch into larvae. This takes from one to ten days. Larvae are not particularly mobile and will usually travel only a few inches from where they hatch. However, they do have a tendency to move away from bright light and heavy

EN GARDE:
CATCHING FLEAS OFF GUARD!

Consider the following ways to arm yourself against fleas:

- Add a small amount of pennyroyal or eucalyptus oil to your dog's bath. These natural remedies repel fleas.
- Supplement your dog's food with fresh garlic (minced or grated) and a hearty amount of brewer's yeast, both of which ward off fleas.
- Use a flea comb on your dog daily. Submerge fleas in a cup of bleach to kill them quickly.
- Confine the dog to only a few rooms to limit the spread of fleas in the home.
- Vacuum daily...and get all of the crevices! Dispose of the bag every few days until the problem is under control.
- Wash your dog's bedding daily. Cover cushions where your dog sleeps with towels, and wash the towels often.

traffic—under furniture and behind doors are common places to find high quantities of flea larvae.

The flea larvae feed on dead organic matter, including adult flea feces, until they are ready to change into adult fleas. Fleas will usually remain as larvae for around seven days. After this period, the larvae will pupate into protective pupae. While inside the pupae, the larvae will undergo metamorphosis and change into

Fleas have been measured as being able to jump 300,000 times and can jump over 150 times their length in any direction, including straight up.

adult fleas. This can take as little time as a few days, but the adult fleas can remain inside the pupae waiting to hatch for up to two years. The pupae are signaled to hatch by certain stimuli, such as physical pressure—the pupae's being stepped on, heat from an animal's lying on the pupae or increased carbon-dioxide levels and vibrations—indicating that a suitable host is available.

Once hatched, the adult flea must feed within a few days. Once the adult flea finds a host, it will not leave voluntarily. It only becomes dislodged by grooming or the host animal's scratching. The adult flea will remain on the

PHOTO BY DWIGHT R. KUHN

host for the duration of its life unless forcibly removed.

TREATING THE ENVIRONMENT AND THE DOG

Treating fleas should be a two-pronged attack. First, the environment needs to be treated; this includes carpets and furniture, especially the dog's bedding and areas underneath furniture. The environment should be treated with a household spray containing an Insect Growth Regulator (IGR) and an insecticide to kill the adult fleas. Most IGRs are effective against eggs and larvae; they actually mimic the fleas' own hormones and stop the eggs and larvae from developing into adult fleas. There are currently no treatments available to attack the pupa stage of the life cycle, so the adult insecticide is used to kill the newly hatched adult fleas before they find a host. Most IGRs are active for many months, while adult insecticides are only active

A scanning electron micrograph of a dog or cat flea, *Ctenocephalides*, magnified more than 100x. This image has been colorized for effect.

S. E. M. BY DR. DENNIS KUNKEL, UNIVERSITY OF HAWAII

THE LIFE CYCLE OF THE FLEA

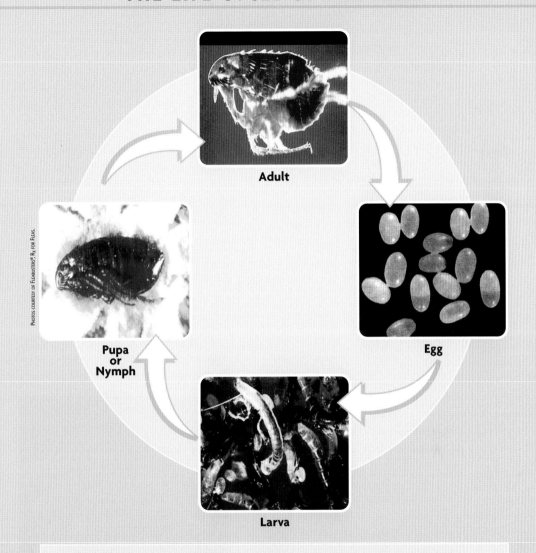

Adult

Egg

Larva

Pupa
or
Nymph

Fleas have been around for millions of years and have adapted to changing host animals. They are able to go through a complete life cycle in less than one month or they can extend their lives to almost two years by remaining as pupae or cocoons. They do not need blood or any other food for up to 20 months.

INSECT GROWTH REGULATOR (IGR)

Two types of products should be used when treating fleas—a product to treat the pet and a product to treat the home. Adult fleas represent less than 1% of the flea population. The pre-adult fleas (eggs, larvae and pupae) represent more than 99% of the flea population and are found in the environment; it is in the case of pre-adult fleas that products containing an Insect Growth Regulator (IGR) should be used in the home.

IGRs are a new class of compounds used to prevent the development of insects. They do not kill the insect outright, but instead use the insect's biology against it to stop it from completing its growth. Products that contain methoprene are the world's first and leading IGRs. Used to control fleas and other insects, this type of IGR will stop flea larvae from developing and protect the house for up to seven months.

for a few days.

When treating with a household spray, it is a good idea to vacuum before applying the product. This stimulates as many pupae as possible to hatch into adult fleas. The vacuum cleaner should also be treated with an insecticide to prevent the eggs and larvae that have been collected in the vacuum bag from hatching.

The second stage of treatment is to apply an adult insecticide to the dog. Traditionally, this would be in the form of a collar or a spray, but more recent innovations include digestible insecticides that poison the fleas when they ingest the dog's blood. Alternatively, there are drops that, when placed on the back of the dog's neck, spread throughout the hair and skin to kill adult fleas.

TICKS

Though not as common as fleas, ticks are found all over the tropical and temperate world. They don't bite, like fleas; they harpoon. They dig their sharp proboscis (nose) into the dog's skin and drink the blood. Their only food and drink is dog's

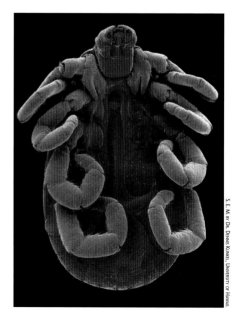

S. E. M. by Dr. Dennis Kunkel, University of Hawaii

blood. Dogs can get Lyme disease, Rocky Mountain spotted fever, tick bite paralysis and many other diseases from ticks. They may live where fleas are found and they like to hide in cracks or seams in walls. They are controlled the same way fleas are controlled.

The American dog tick, *Dermacentor variabilis*, may well be the most common dog tick in many geographical areas, especially those areas where the climate is hot and humid. Most dog ticks have life expectancies of a week to six months, depending upon climatic conditions. They can neither jump nor fly, but they can crawl slowly and can range up to 16 feet to reach a sleeping or unsuspecting dog.

MITES

Just as fleas and ticks can be problematic for your dog, mites can also lead to an itchy nuisance. Microscopic in size, mites are related to ticks and generally take up permanent residence on their host animal—in this case, your dog! The term *mange* refers to any infestation caused by one of the mighty mites, of which there are six varieties that concern dog owners.

Demodex mites cause a condition known as demodicosis (sometimes called red mange or

DEER-TICK CROSSING

The great outdoors may be fun for your dog, but it also is a home to dangerous ticks. Deer ticks carry a bacterium known as *Borrelia burgdorferi* and are most active in the autumn and spring. When infections are caught early, penicillin and tetracycline are effective antibiotics, but, if left untreated, the bacteria may cause neurological, kidney and cardiac problems as well as long-term trouble with walking and painful joints.

The head of an American dog tick, *Dermacentor variabilis,* enlarged and colorized for effect.

The mange mite, *Psoroptes bovis*, can infest cattle and other domestic animals.

Photo by James Hayden/Yoav/Phototake.

follicular mange), in which the mites live in the dog's hair follicles and sebaceous glands in larger-than-normal numbers. This type of mange is commonly passed from the dam to her puppies and usually shows up on the puppies' muzzles, though demodicosis is not transferable from one normal dog to another. Most dogs recover from this type of mange without any treatment, though topical therapies are commonly prescribed by the vet.

Human lice look like dog lice; the two are closely related.

Photo by Dwight R. Kuhn.

The *Cheyletiellosis* mite is the hook-mouthed culprit associated with "walking dandruff," a condition that affects dogs as well as cats and rabbits. This mite lives on the surface of the animal's skin and is readily transferable through direct or indirect contact with an affected animal. The dandruff is present in the form of scaly skin, which may or may not be itchy. If not treated, this mange can affect a whole kennel of dogs and can be spread to humans as well.

The *Sarcoptes* mite causes intense itching on the dog in the form of a condition known as scabies or sarcoptic mange. The cycle of the *Sarcoptes* mite lasts about three weeks, and the mites live in the top layer of the dog's skin (epidermis), preferably in areas with little hair. Scabies is highly contagious and can be passed to humans. Sometimes an allergic reaction to the mite worsens the severe itching associated with sarcoptic mange.

Ear mites, *Otodectes cynotis,* lead to otodectic mange, which most commonly affects the outer ear canal of the dog, though other areas can be affected as well. Dogs with ear-mite infestation commonly scratch at their ears, causing further irritation, and shake their heads. Dark brown droppings in the outer ear confirm the diagnosis. Your vet can prescribe a treatment to flush out the ears and kill any eggs in the ears. A complete month of treatment is necessary to cure the mange.

Two other mites, less common in dogs, include *Dermanyssus gallinae* (the poultry or red mite) and *Eutrombicula alfreddugesi* (the North American mite associated with trombiculidiasis or chigger infestation). The poultry mite frequently lives on chickens, but can transfer to dogs who spend time near farm animals. Chigger infestation affects dogs in the

DO NOT MIX
Never mix parasite-control products without first consulting your vet. Some products can become toxic when combined with others and can cause fatal consequences.

NOT A DROP TO DRINK
Never allow your dog to swim in polluted water or public areas where water quality can be suspect. Even perfectly clear water can harbor parasites, many of which can cause serious to fatal illnesses in canines. Areas inhabited by waterfowl and other wildlife are especially dangerous.

Central US who have exposure to woodlands. The types of mange caused by both of these mites are treatable by vets.

INTERNAL PARASITES
Most animals—fishes, birds and mammals, including dogs and humans—have worms and other parasites that live inside their bodies. According to Dr. Herbert R. Axelrod, the fish pathologist, there are two kinds of parasites: dumb and smart. The smart parasites live in peaceful cooperation with their hosts (symbiosis), while the dumb parasites kill their hosts. Most worm infections are relatively easy to control. If they are not controlled, they weaken the host dog to the point that other medical problems occur, but they do not kill the host as dumb parasites would.

A brown dog tick, *Rhipicephalus sanguineus*, is an uncommon but annoying tick found on dogs.
PHOTO BY CAROLINA BIOLOGICAL SUPPLY/PHOTOTAKE.

The roundworm *Rhabditis* can infect both dogs and humans.

The roundworm, *Ascaris lumbricoides*.

ROUNDWORMS

Average-size dogs can pass 1,360,000 roundworm eggs every day. For example, if there were only 1 million dogs in the world, the world would be saturated with thousands of tons of dog feces. These feces would contain around 15,000,000,000 roundworm eggs.

Up to 31% of home yards and children's sand boxes in the US contain roundworm eggs.

Flushing dog's feces down the toilet is not a safe practice because the usual sewage treatments do not destroy roundworm eggs.

Infected puppies start shedding roundworm eggs at three weeks of age. They can be infected by their mother's milk.

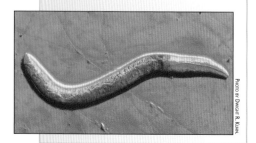

ROUNDWORMS

The roundworms that infect dogs are known scientifically as *Toxocara canis*. They live in the dog's intestines and shed eggs continually. It has been estimated that a dog produces about 6 or more ounces of feces every day. Each ounce of feces averages hundreds of thousands of roundworm eggs. There are no known areas in which dogs roam that do not contain roundworm eggs. The greatest danger of roundworms is that they infect people, too! It is wise to have your dog tested regularly for roundworms.

In young puppies, roundworms cause bloated bellies, diarrhea, coughing and vomiting, and are transmitted from the dam (through blood or milk). Affected puppies will not appear as animated as normal puppies. The worms appear spaghetti-like, measuring as long as 6 inches. Adult dogs can acquire roundworms through coprophagia (eating contaminated feces) or by killing rodents that carry roundworms.

Roundworm infection can kill puppies and cause severe problems in adults, as the hatched larvae travel to the lungs and trachea through the bloodstream. Cleanliness is the best preventative for roundworms. Always pick up after your dog and dispose of feces in appropriate receptacles.

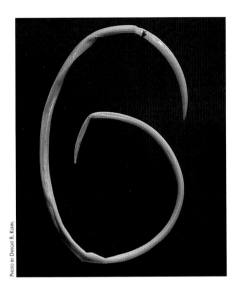

Photo by Dwight R. Kuhl.

HOOKWORMS

In the United States, dog owners have to be concerned about four different species of hookworm, the most common and most serious of which is *Ancylostoma caninum*, which prefers warm climates. The others are *Ancylostoma braziliense, Ancylostoma tubaeforme* and *Uncinaria stenocephala,* the latter of which is a concern to dogs living in the Northern US and Canada, as this species prefers cold climates.

Hookworms are dangerous to humans as well as to dogs and cats, and can be the cause of severe anemia due to iron deficiency. The worm uses its teeth to attach itself to the dog's intestines and changes the site of its attachment about six times per day. Each time the worm reposi-

tions itself, the dog loses blood and can become anemic. *Ancylostoma caninum* is the most likely of the four species to cause anemia in the dog.

Symptoms of hookworm infection include dark stools, weight loss, general weakness, pale coloration and anemia, as well as possible skin problems. Fortunately, hookworms are easily purged from the affected dog with a number of medications that have proven effective. Discuss these with your vet. Most heartworm preventatives include a hookworm insecticide as well.

Owners also must be aware that hookworms can infect humans, who can acquire the larvae through exposure to contaminated feces. Since the worms cannot complete their life cycle on a human, the worms simply infest the skin and cause irritation. This condition is known as cutaneous larva migrans syndrome. As a preventative, use disposable gloves or a "poop-scoop" to pick up your dog's droppings and prevent your dog (or neighborhood cats) from defecating in children's play areas.

The hookworm, *Ancylostoma caninum.*

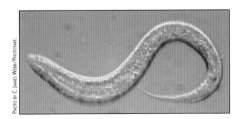

Photo by C. James Webb/Phototake.

The infective stage of the hookworm larva.

TAPEWORMS

Humans, rats, squirrels, foxes, coyotes, wolves and domestic dogs are all susceptible to tapeworm infection. Except in humans, tapeworms are usually not a fatal infection. Infected individuals can harbor 1000 parasitic worms.

Tapeworms, like some other types of worm, are hermaphroditic, meaning male and female in the same worm.

If dogs eat infected rats or mice, or anything else infected with tapeworm, they get the tapeworm disease. One month after attaching to a dog's intestine, the worm starts shedding eggs. These eggs are infective immediately. Infective eggs can live for a few months without a host animal.

The head and rostellum (the round prominence on the scolex) of a tapeworm, which infects dogs and humans.

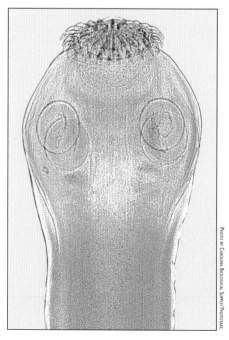

PHOTO BY CAROLINA BIOLOGICAL SUPPLY/PHOTOTAKE

TAPEWORMS

There are many species of tapeworm, all of which are carried by fleas! The most common tapeworm affecting dogs is known as *Dipylidium caninum*. The dog eats the flea and starts the tapeworm cycle. Humans can also be infected with tapeworms—so don't eat fleas! Fleas are so small that your dog could pass them onto your hands, your plate or your food and thus make it possible for you to ingest a flea that is carrying tapeworm eggs.

While tapeworm infection is not life-threatening in dogs (smart parasite!), it can be the cause of a very serious liver disease for humans. About 50% of the humans infected with *Echinococcus multilocularis*, a type of tapeworm that causes alveolar hydatid, perish.

WHIPWORMS

In North America, whipworms are counted among the most common parasitic worms in dogs. The whipworm's scientific name is *Trichuris vulpis*. These worms attach themselves in the lower parts of the intestine, where they feed. Affected dogs may only experience upset tummies, colic and diarrhea. These worms, however, can live for months or years in the dog, beginning their larval stage in the small intestine, spending their adult stage in the large intestine and finally passing infective eggs through the dog's feces. The only way to detect whipworms is through a fecal examination, though this is not always foolproof. Treatment for whipworms is tricky, due to the worms' unusual life-cycle pattern, and very often dogs are reinfected due to exposure to infective eggs on the ground. The whipworm eggs can survive in the environment for as long as five years; thus, cleaning up droppings in your own backyard as well as in public places is absolutely essential for sanitation purposes and the health of your dog and others.

THREADWORMS

Though less common than roundworms, hookworms and those previously mentioned, threadworms concern dog owners in the southwestern US and Gulf Coast area where the climate is hot and humid. Living in the small intestine of the dog, this worm measures a mere 2 millimeters and is round in shape. Like that of the whipworm, the threadworm's life cycle is very complex and the eggs and larvae are passed through the feces. A deadly disease in humans, *Strongyloides* readily infects people, and the handling of feces is the most common means of transmission. Threadworms are most often seen in young puppies; bloody diarrhea and pneumonia are symptoms. Sick puppies must be isolated and treated immediately; vets recommend a follow-up treatment one month later.

HEARTWORM PREVENTATIVES

There are many heartworm preventatives on the market, many of which are sold at your veterinarian's office. These products can be given daily or monthly, depending on the manufacturer's instructions. All of these preventatives contain chemical insecticides directed at killing heartworms, which leads to some controversy among dog owners. In effect, heartworm preventatives are necessary evils, though you should determine how necessary based on your pet's lifestyle. There is no doubt that heartworm is a dreadful disease that threatens the lives of dogs. However, the likelihood of your dog's being bitten by an infected mosquito is slim in most places, and a mosquito-repellent (or an herbal remedy such as Wormwood or Black Walnut) is much safer for your dog and will not compromise his immune system (the way heartworm preventatives will). Should you decide to use the traditional preventative "medications," you can consider giving the pill every other or third month. Since the toxins in the pill will kill the heartworms at all stages of development, the pill would be effective in killing larvae, nymphs or adults, and it takes four months for the larvae to reach the adult stage. Thus, there is no rationale to poisoning the dog's system on a monthly basis. Lastly, do not give the pill during the winter months since there are no mosquitoes around to pass on their infection, unless you live in a tropical environment.

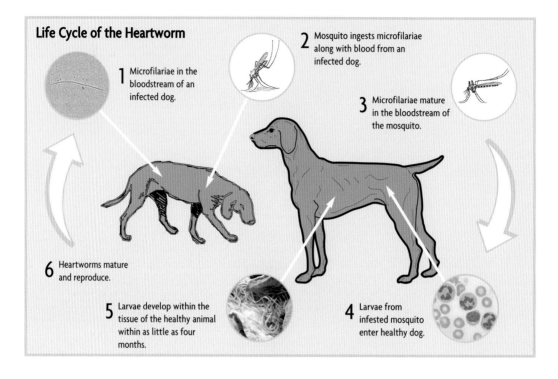

Life Cycle of the Heartworm

1 Microfilariae in the bloodstream of an infected dog.

2 Mosquito ingests microfilariae along with blood from an infected dog.

3 Microfilariae mature in the bloodstream of the mosquito.

4 Larvae from infested mosquito enter healthy dog.

5 Larvae develop within the tissue of the healthy animal within as little as four months.

6 Heartworms mature and reproduce.

HEARTWORMS

Heartworms are thin, extended worms up to 12 inches long, which live in a dog's heart and the major blood vessels surrounding it. Dogs may have up to 200 worms. Symptoms may be loss of energy, loss of appetite, coughing, the development of a pot belly and anemia.

Heartworms are transmitted by mosquitoes. The mosquito drinks the blood of an infected dog and takes in larvae with the blood. The larvae, called microfilariae, develop within the body of the mosquito and are passed on to the next dog bitten after the larvae mature. It takes two to three weeks for the larvae to develop to the infective stage within the body of the mosquito. Dogs are usually treated at about six weeks of age and maintained on a prophylactic dose given monthly.

Blood testing for heartworms is not necessarily indicative of how seriously your dog is infected. Although this is a dangerous disease, it is not easy for a dog to be infected. Discuss the various preventatives with your vet, as there are many different types now available. Together you can decide on a safe course of prevention for your dog.

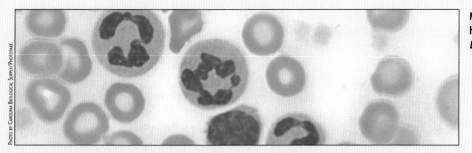

Magnified heartworm larvae, *Dirofilaria immitis.*

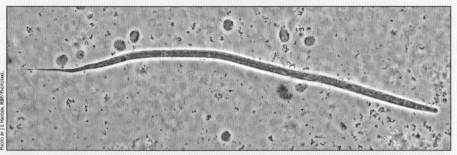

Heartworm, *Dirofilaria immitis.*

The heart of a dog infected with canine heartworm, *Dirofilaria immitis.*

HOMEOPATHY:
an alternative to conventional medicine

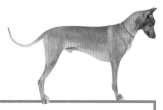

"Less is Most"

Using this principle, the strength of a homeopathic remedy is measured by the number of serial dilutions that were undertaken to create it. The greater the number of serial dilutions, the greater the strength of the homeopathic remedy. The potency of a remedy that has been made by making a dilution of 1 part in 100 parts (or 1/100) is 1c or 1cH. If this remedy is subjected to a series of further dilutions, each one being 1/100, a more dilute and stronger remedy is produced. If the remedy is diluted in this way six times, it is called 6c or 6cH. A dilution of 6c is 1 part in 1,000,000,000,000. In general, higher potencies in more frequent doses are better for acute symptoms and lower potencies in more infrequent doses are more useful for chronic, long-standing problems.

CURING OUR DOGS NATURALLY

Holistic medicine means treating the whole animal as a unique, perfect, living being. Generally, holistic treatments do not suppress the symptoms that the body naturally produces, as do most medications prescribed by conventional doctors and vets. Holistic methods seek to cure disease by regaining balance and harmony in the patient's environment. Some of these methods include use of nutritional therapy, herbs, flower essences, aromatherapy, acupuncture, massage, chiropractic and, of course, the most popular holistic approach, homeopathy.

Homeopathy is a theory or system of treating illness with small doses of substances which, if administered in larger quantities, would produce the symptoms that the patient already has. This approach is often described as "like cures like." Although modern veterinary medicine is geared toward the "quick fix," homeopathy relies on the belief that, given the time, the body is able to heal itself and return to its natural, healthy state.

Choosing a remedy to cure a problem in our dogs is the difficult part of homeopathy. Consult with your vet for a professional diagnosis of your dog's symptoms. Often these symptoms require

immediate conventional care. If your vet is willing and knowledgeable, you may attempt a homeopathic remedy. Be aware that cortisone prevents homeopathic remedies from working. There are hundreds of possibilities and combinations to cure many problems in dogs, from basic physical problems such as excessive shedding, fleas or other parasites, unattractive doggy odor, bad breath, upset tummy, obesity, dry, oily or dull coat, diarrhea, ear problems or eye discharge (including tears and dry or mucousy matter), to behavioral abnormalities such as fear of loud noises, habitual licking, poor appetite, excessive barking and various phobias. From alumina to zincum metallicum, the remedies span the planet and the imagination…from flowers and weeds to chemicals, insect droppings, diesel smoke and volcanic ash.

Using "Like to Treat Like"

Unlike conventional medicines that suppress symptoms, homeopathic remedies treat illnesses with small doses of substances that, if administered in larger quantities, would produce the symptoms that the patient already has. While the same homeopathic remedy can be used to treat different symptoms in different dogs, here are some interesting remedies and their uses.

Apis Mellifica

(made from honey bee venom) can be used for allergies or to reduce swelling that occurs in acutely infected kidneys.

Diesel Smoke

can be used to help control travel sickness.

Calcarea Fluorica

(made from calcium fluoride, which helps harden bone structure) can be useful in treating hard lumps in tissues.

Natrum Muriaticum

(made from common salt, sodium chloride) is useful in treating thin, thirsty dogs.

Nitricum Acidum

(made from nitric acid) is used for symptoms you would expect to see from contact with acids, such as lesions, especially where the skin joins the linings of body orifices or openings such as the lips and nostrils.

Symphytum

(made from the herb Knitbone, *Symphytum officianale*) is used to encourage bones to heal.

Urtica Urens

(made from the common stinging nettle) is used in treating painful, irritating rashes.

HOMEOPATHIC REMEDIES FOR YOUR DOG

Symptom/Ailment	Possible Remedy
ALLERGIES	Apis Mellifica 30c, Astacus Fluviatilis 6c, Pulsatilla 30c, Urtica Urens 6c
ALOPECIA	Alumina 30c, Lycopodium 30c, Sepia 30c, Thallium 6c
ANAL GLANDS (BLOCKED)	Hepar Sulphuris Calcareum 30c, Sanicula 6c, Silicea 6c
ARTHRITIS	Rhus Toxicodendron 6c, Bryonia Alba 6c
CANINE COUGH	Drosera 6c, Ipecacuanha 30c
CATARACT	Calcarea Carbonica 6c, Conium Maculatum 6c, Phosphorus 30c, Silicea 30c
CONSTIPATION	Alumina 6c, Carbo Vegetabilis 30c, Graphites 6c, Nitricum Acidum 30c, Silicea 6c
COUGHING	Aconitum Napellus 6c, Belladonna 30c, Hyoscyamus Niger 30c, Phosphorus 30c
DIARRHEA	Arsenicum Album 30c, Aconitum Napellus 6c, Chamomilla 30c, Mercurius Corrosivus 30c
DRY EYE	Zincum Metallicum 30c
EAR PROBLEMS	Aconitum Napellus 30c, Belladonna 30c, Hepar Sulphuris 30c, Tellurium 30c, Psorinum 200c
EYE PROBLEMS	Borax 6c, Aconitum Napellus 30c, Graphites 6c, Staphysagria 6c, Thuja Occidentalis 30c
GLAUCOMA	Aconitum Napellus 30c, Apis Mellifica 6c, Phosphorus 30c
HEAT STROKE	Belladonna 30c, Gelsemium Sempervirens 30c, Sulphur 30c
HICCOUGHS	Cinchona Deficinalis 6c
HIP DYSPLASIA	Colocynthis 6c, Rhus Toxicodendron 6c, Bryonia Alba 6c
INCONTINENCE	Argentum Nitricum 6c, Causticum 30c, Conium Maculatum 30c, Pulsatilla 30c, Sepia 30c
INSECT BITES	Apis Mellifica 30c, Cantharis 30c, Hypericum Perforatum 6c, Urtica Urens 30c
ITCHING	Alumina 30c, Arsenicum Album 30c, Carbo Vegetabilis 30c, Hypericum Perforatum 6c, Mezerium 6c, Sulphur 30c
MASTITIS	Apis Mellifica 30c, Belladonna 30c, Urtica Urens 1m
MOTION SICKNESS	Cocculus 6c, Petroleum 6c
PATELLAR LUXATION	Gelsemium Sempervirens 6c, Rhus Toxicodendron 6c
PENIS PROBLEMS	Aconitum Napellus 30c, Hepar Sulphuris Calcareum 30c, Pulsatilla 30c, Thuja Occidentalis 6c
PUPPY TEETHING	Calcarea Carbonica 6c, Chamomilla 6c, Phytolacca 6c

Recognizing a Sick Dog

Unlike colicky babies and cranky children, our canine kids cannot tell us when they are feeling ill. Therefore, there are a number of signs that owners can identify to know that their dogs are not feeling well.

Take note for physical manifestations such as:

- unusual, bad odor, including bad breath
- excessive shedding
- wax in the ears, chronic ear irritation
- oily, flaky, dull haircoat
- mucus, tearing or similar discharge in the eyes
- fleas or mites
- mucus in stool, diarrhea
- sensitivity to petting or handling
- licking at paws, scratching face, etc.

Keep an eye out for behavioral changes as well, including:

- lethargy, idleness
- lack of patience or general irritability
- lack of interest in food
- phobias (fear of people, loud noises, etc.)
- strange behavior, suspicion, fear
- coprophagia
- more frequent barking
- whimpering, crying

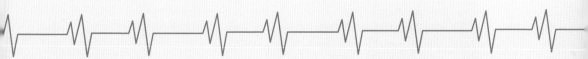

Get Well Soon

You don't need a DVM to provide good TLC to your sick or recovering dog, but you do need to pay attention to some details that normally wouldn't bother him. The following tips will aid Fido's recovery and get him back on his paws again:

- Keep his space free of irritating smells, like heavy perfumes and air fresheners.
- Rest is the best medicine! Avoid harsh lighting that will prevent your dog from sleeping. Shade him from bright sunlight during the day and dim the lights in the evening.
- Keep the noise level down. Animals are more sensitive to sound when they are sick.

- Be attentive to any necessary temperature adjustments. A dog with a fever needs a cool room and cold liquids. A bitch that is whelping or recovering from surgery will be more comfortable in a warm room, consuming warm liquids and food.
- You wouldn't send a sick child back to school early, so don't rush your dog back into a full routine until he seems absolutely ready.

Show dogs are gaited in the ring so that the judge can evaluate the dog's movement. Proper structure leads to proper movement, and this is important in a quick, agile sighthound breed.

SHOWING YOUR
PHARAOH HOUND

When you purchase your Pharaoh Hound, you will make it clear to the breeder whether you want one just as a lovable companion and pet, or if you hope to be buying a Pharaoh Hound with show prospects. No reputable breeder will sell you a young puppy and tell you that it is *definitely* of show quality, for so much can go wrong during the early months of a puppy's development. If you plan to show, what you will hopefully have acquired is a puppy with "show potential." To the novice, exhibiting a Pharaoh Hound in the show ring may look easy, but it takes a lot of hard work and devotion to do top winning at a show such as the prestigious Westminster Kennel Club dog show, not to mention a little luck too!

The first concept that the canine novice learns when watching a dog show is that each dog first competes against members of his own breed. Once the judge has selected the best member of each breed (Best of Breed), provided that the show is judged on a Group system, that chosen dog will compete with other dogs in his group. Finally,

the dogs chosen first in each group will compete for Best in Show.

The second concept that you must understand is that the dogs are not actually compared against one another. The judge compares each dog against his breed standard, the written description of the ideal specimen that is approved by the American Kennel Club (AKC). While some early breed standards were indeed based on specific dogs that were famous or popular, many dedicated enthusiasts say that a perfect specimen, as described in the standard, has never walked into a show ring, has never been bred and, to the woe of dog breeders around the globe, does not exist. Breeders attempt to get as close to this ideal as possible with every litter, but theoretically

As the judge looks over the line-up, she mentally compares each dog to the ideal set forth in the breed standard.

The judge performs a hands-on examination of each dog, feeling for correct body construction and soundness. This includes opening the dog's mouth to check the bite and dentition.

The judge performs a hands-on examination of each dog, feeling for correct body construction and soundness. This includes opening the dog's mouth to check the bite and dentition.

the "perfect" dog is so elusive that it is impossible. (And if the "perfect" dog were born, breeders and judges would never agree that it was indeed "perfect.")

If you are interested in exploring the world of dog showing, your best bet is to join your local breed club or the national parent club, which is the Pharaoh Hound Club of America. These clubs often host both regional and national specialties, shows only for Pharaoh Hounds, which can include conformation as well as obedience and agility trials and lure coursing. Even if you have no intention of competing with your Pharaoh

Hound, a specialty is like a festival for lovers of the breed who congregate to share their favorite topic: Pharaoh Hounds! Clubs also send out newsletters, and some organize training days and seminars in order that people may learn more about their chosen breed. To locate the breed club closest to you, contact the AKC, which furnishes the rules and regulations for all of these events plus general dog registration and other basic requirements of dog ownership.

The AKC offers three kinds of conformation shows: An all-breed show (for all recognized breeds), a specialty show (for one breed only, usually sponsored by the parent club) and a group show (for all breeds in the Group).

For a dog to become an AKC champion of record, the dog must accumulate 15 points at shows from at least three different judges, including two "majors." A "major" is defined as a three-, four- or five-point win, and the number of points per win is determined by the number of dogs entered in the show on that day. Depending on the breed, the number of points that are awarded varies. In numerically strong breeds, more dogs are needed to rack up the points; the opposite is true for less popular breeds. At any dog show, only one dog and one bitch of each breed can win points.

Dog showing does not offer "co-ed" classes. Dogs and bitches

Still going strong! Despite the gray muzzle, this senior canine citizen continues to rack up wins in the show ring.

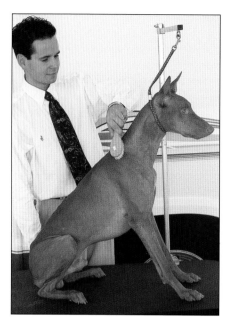

A quick once-over before appearing in the ring gives the Pharaoh Hound's coat a lustrous shine so that he will sparkle for the judge.

US) and the Open Class (for any dog that is not a champion).

The judge at the show begins judging the Puppy Class, first dogs and then bitches, and proceeds through the classes. The judge places his winners first through fourth in each class. In the Winners Class, the first-place winners of each class compete with one another to determine Winners Dog and Winners Bitch. The judge also places a Reserve Winners Dog and Reserve Winners Bitch, which could be awarded the points in the case of a disqualification. The Winners Dog and Winners Bitch, the two that are awarded the points for the breed, then compete with any champions of record entered in the show, which are usually called "specials." The judge reviews the Winners Dog, Winners Bitch and all of the champions to select his Best of Breed. The Best of Winners is selected between the Winners Dog and Winners Bitch. Were one of these two to be selected Best of Breed, he or she would automatically be named Best of Winners as well. Finally the judge selects his Best of Opposite Sex to the Best of Breed winner.

At a Group show or all-breed show, the Best of Breed winners from each breed then compete against one another for Group One through Group Four. The judge compares each Best of Breed to

never compete against each other in the classes. Non-champion dogs are called "class dogs" because they compete in one of five classes. Dogs are entered in a particular class depending on his age and previous show wins. To begin, there is the Puppy Class (for 6- to 9-month-olds and for 9- to 12-month-olds); this class is followed by the Novice Class (for dogs that have not won any first prizes except in the Puppy Class or three first prizes in the Novice Class and have not accumulated any points toward their champion title); the Bred-by-Exhibitor Class (for dogs handled by their breeders or one of the breeder's immediate family); the American-bred Class (for dogs bred in the

his breed standard, and the dog that most closely lives up to the ideal for his breed is selected as Group One. Finally, all seven group winners (from the Hound Group, Toy Group, Working Group, etc.) compete for Best in Show.

To find out about dog shows in your area, you can subscribe to the American Kennel Club's monthly magazine, The *American Kennel Gazette* and the accompanying *Events Calendar*. You can also look in your local newspaper for advertisements for dog shows in your area or go to the AKC's website, www.akc.org.

If your Pharaoh Hound is six months of age or older and registered with the AKC, you can enter him in a dog show where the breed is offered classes. Provided that your Pharaoh Hound does not have a disqualifying fault, he can compete. Only unaltered dogs can be entered in a dog show, so if you have spayed or neutered your Pharaoh Hound, your dog cannot compete in conformation shows. The reason for this is simple. Dog shows are the main forum to prove which representatives of a breed are worthy of being bred. Only dogs that have achieved championships—the AKC "seal of approval" for quality in pure-bred dogs—should be bred. Altered dogs, however, can participate in other AKC events such as

obedience trials and the Canine Good Citizen® program.

Before you actually step into the ring, you would be well advised to sit back and observe the judge's ring procedure. If it is your first time in the ring, do not be over-anxious and run to the front of the line. It is much better to stand back and study how the exhibitor in front of you is performing. The judge asks each handler to "stack" the dog, hopefully showing the dog off to his best advantage. The judge will observe the dog from a distance and from different angles, and approach the dog to check his teeth, overall structure, alertness and muscle tone, as well as consider how well the dog "conforms" to the standard. Most importantly, the judge will have the exhibitor move the dog around the ring in some pattern that he should specify (another advantage to not going first, but always listen since some judges

AKC GROUPS

For showing purposes, the American Kennel Club divides its recognized breeds into seven groups: Hounds, Sporting Dogs, Working Dogs, Terriers, Toys, Non-Sporting Dogs and Herding Dogs.

change their directions—and the judge is always right!). Finally, the judge will give the dog one last look before moving on to the next exhibitor.

If you are not in the top four in your class at your first show, do not be discouraged. Be patient and consistent, and you may eventually find yourself in a winning line-up. Remember that the winners were once in your shoes and have devoted many hours and much money to earn the placement. If you find that your dog is losing every time and never getting a nod, it may be time to consider a different dog sport or to just enjoy your Pharaoh Hound as a pet. Parent clubs offer other events, such as lure coursing, agility, tracking, obedience, instinct tests and more, which may be of interest to the owner of a well-trained Pharaoh Hound.

OBEDIENCE TRIALS
Obedience trials in the US trace back to the early 1930s when organized obedience training was developed to demonstrate how well dog and owner could work together. The pioneer of obedience trials is Mrs. Helen Whitehouse Walker, a Standard Poodle fancier, who designed a series of exercises after the Associated Sheep, Police, Army Dog Society of Great Britain. Since the days of Mrs. Walker, obedience trials have grown by leaps and bounds, and today there are over 2,000 trials held in the US every year, with more than 100,000 dogs competing. Any registered AKC dog can enter an obedience trial, regardless of conformational disqualifications or neutering.

Obedience trials are divided into three levels of progressive difficulty. At the first level, the Novice, dogs compete for the title Companion Dog (CD); at the intermediate level, the Open, dogs compete for the title Companion Dog Excellent (CDX); and at the advanced level, the Utility, dogs compete for the title Utility Dog (UD). Classes are sub-divided into "A" (for beginners) and "B" (for more experienced handlers). A perfect score at any level is 200, and a dog must score 170 or better to earn a "leg," of which three are needed to earn the title. To earn points, the dog must score more than 50% of the available points in each exercise; the possible points range from 20 to 40.

TEMPERAMENT PLUS
Although it seems that physical conformation is the only factor considered in the show ring, temperament is also of utmost importance. An aggressive or fearful dog should not be shown, as bad behavior will not be tolerated and may pose a threat to the judge, other exhibitors, you and your dog.

Each level consists of a different set of exercises. In the Novice level, the dog must heel on- and off-lead, come, long sit, long down and stand for examination. These skills are the basic ones required for a well-behaved "Companion Dog." The Open level requires that the dog perform the same exercises as mentioned but without a leash for extended lengths of time, as well as retrieve a dumbbell, broad jump and drop on recall. In the Utility level, dogs must perform ten difficult exercises, including scent discrimination, hand signals for basic commands, directed jump and directed retrieve.

Once a dog has earned the UD title, he can compete with other proven obedience dogs for the coveted title of Utility Dog Excellent (UDX), which requires that the dog win "legs" in ten shows. Utility Dogs who earn "legs" in Open B and Utility B earn points toward their Obedience Trial Champion title. In 1977, the title Obedience Trial Champion (OTCh.) was established by the AKC. To become an OTCh., a dog needed to earn 100 points, which requires three first places in Open B and Utility under three different judges.

The Grand Prix of obedience trials, the AKC National Obedience Invitational gives qualifying Utility Dogs the chance

CLUB CONTACTS

You can get information about dog shows from the national kennel clubs:

American Kennel Club
5580 Centerview Dr., Raleigh, NC 27606-3390
www.akc.org

United Kennel Club
100 E. Kilgore Road, Kalamazoo, MI 49002
www.ukcdogs.com

Canadian Kennel Club
89 Skyway Ave., Suite 100, Etobicoke, Ontario
M9W 6R4, Canada
www.ckc.ca

The Kennel Club
1-5 Clarges St., Piccadilly, London
W1Y 8AB, UK
www.the-kennel-club.org.uk

to win the newest and highest title: National Obedience Champion (NOC). Only the top 25 ranked obedience dogs, plus any dog ranked in the top 3 in his breed, are allowed to compete.

AGILITY TRIALS

Having had its origins in the UK back in 1977, AKC agility had its official beginning in the US in August 1994, when the first licensed agility trials were held. The AKC allows all registered breeds (including Miscellaneous Class breeds) to participate, providing the dog is 12 months of age or older. Agility is designed so that the handler demonstrates how well the dog can work at his side. The handler directs his dog over an obstacle course that includes jumps as well as tires, the dog walk, weave poles, pipe tunnels, collapsed tunnels, etc. While working his way through the course, the dog must keep one eye and ear on the handler and the rest of his body on the course. The handler gives verbal and hand signals to guide the dog through the course.

The first organization to promote agility trials in the US was the United States Dog Agility Association, Inc. (USDAA), which was established in 1986 and spawned numerous member clubs around the country. Both the USDAA and the AKC offer titles to winning dogs. Three titles are available through the USDAA: Agility Dog (AD), Advanced Agility Dog (AAD) and Master

Dogs are trained for the long jump by gradually adding boards to extend the length that the dog must jump.

Agility Dog (MAD). The AKC offers Novice Agility (NA), Open Agility (OA), Agility Excellent (AX) and Master Agility Excellent (MX). Beyond these four AKC titles, dogs can win additional ones in "jumper" classes, Jumpers with Weave Novice (NAJ), Open (OAJ) and Excellent (MXJ), which lead to the ultimate title(s): MACH, Master Agility Champion. Dogs can continue to add number designations to the MACH titles, indicating how many times the dog has met the MACH requirements, such as MACH1, MACH2, and so on.

Agility is great fun for dog and owner with many rewards for everyone involved. If you are interested in giving it a try, you should join a training club that has obstacles and experienced agility handlers who can introduce you and your dog to the "ropes" (and tires, tunnels, etc.).

TRACKING
Any dog is capable of tracking, using his nose to follow a trail. Tracking tests are exciting and competitive ways to test your Pharaoh Hound's keen nose and ability to search and rescue. The AKC started tracking tests in 1937, when the first AKC-licensed test took place as a part of the Utility level at an obedience trial. Ten years later in 1947, the AKC offered the first title, Tracking Dog (TD). It was not until 1980 that the AKC added the title Tracking Dog Excellent (TDX), which was followed by the title Versatile Surface Tracking (VST) in 1995. The title Champion Tracker (CT) is awarded to a dog who has earned all three titles.

In the beginning level of tracking, the owner follows the dog through a field on a long leash. To earn the TD title, the dog must follow a track laid by a human 30 to 120 minutes prior. The track is about 500 yards with up to 5 directional changes. The TDX requires that the dog follow a track that is 3 to 5 hours old over a course up to 1,000 yards with up to 7 directional changes. The VST requires that the dog follow a track up to 5 hours old through an urban setting.

LURE COURSING
AKC lure-coursing events are open to all members of the sighthound family, including such breeds as the Scottish Deerhound, Greyhound, Whippet, Irish Wolfhound and, of course, the Pharaoh Hound. Chasing fleet-footed quarry is the born-for function of the Pharaoh Hound, and lure-coursing trials challenge and test the breed's natural instincts. All dogs must be one year of age to compete in these events. For more information on these trials, contact the AKC for their rules and regulations and a schedule of events in your area.

PHARAOH HOUND

As a Pharaoh Hound owner, you have selected your dog so that you and your loved ones can have a companion, a protector, a friend and a four-legged family member. You invest time, money and effort to care for and train the family's new charge. Of course, this chosen canine behaves perfectly! Well, perfectly like a *dog*.

THINK LIKE A DOG

Dogs do not think like humans, nor do humans think like dogs, though we try. Unfortunately, a dog is incapable of comprehending how humans think, so the responsibility falls on the owner to adopt a viable canine mindset. Dogs cannot rationalize, and they exist in the present moment. Many a dog owner makes the mistake in training of thinking that he can reprimand his dog for something the dog did a while ago. Basically, you cannot even reprimand a dog for something he did 20 seconds ago! Either catch him in the act or forget it! It is a waste of your and your dog's time—in his mind, you are reprimanding him for whatever he is doing at that moment.

The following behavioral problems represent some that owners most commonly encounter. Every dog is unique and every situation is unique. No author could purport for you to solve your Pharaoh Hound's problems simply by reading a chapter. Here we outline some basic "dogspeak" so that owners' chances of solving behavioral problems are increased. Discuss bad habits with your veterinarian and he can recommend a behavioral specialist to consult in appropriate cases. Since behavioral abnormalities are the main reason that owners abandon their pets, we hope that you will make a valiant effort to solve your Pharaoh Hound's problems. Patience and understanding are virtues that must dwell in every pet-loving household.

SEPARATION ANXIETY

Your Pharaoh Hound may howl, whine or otherwise vocalize his displeasure at your leaving the house and his being left alone. This is a normal reaction, no different than the child who cries as his mother leaves him on the first day at school. In fact, constant attention can lead to separation anxiety in the first place. If you are constantly making a fuss over your dog, he will come to expect this from you all of the time and it will be more traumatic for him when you are not there. Obviously, you enjoy spending time with your dog, and he thrives on your love and attention. However, it should not become a dependent relationship in which he is heartbroken without you.

One thing you can do to minimize separation anxiety is to make your entrances and exits as low-key as possible. Do not give your dog a long drawn-out goodbye, and do not lavish him with hugs and kisses when you return. This is giving in to the attention that he craves, and it will only make him miss it more when you are away. Another thing you can try is to give your dog a treat when you leave; this will not only keep him occupied and keep his mind off the fact that you have just left, but it will also help him associate your leaving with a pleasant experience.

You may have to accustom your dog to being left alone at intervals. Of course, when your dog starts whimpering as you approach the door, your first instinct will be to run to him and comfort him, but do not do it! Really—eventually he will adjust to your absence. His anxiety

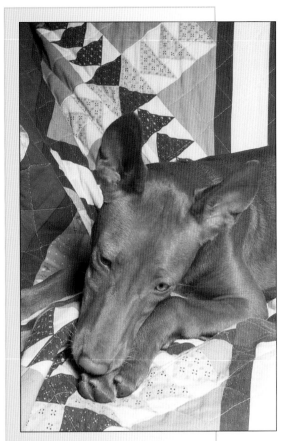

"LONELY WOLF"

The number of dogs that suffer from separation anxiety is on the rise as more and more pet owners find themselves at work all day. New attention is being paid to this problem, which is especially hard to diagnose since it is only evident when the dog is alone. Research is currently being done to help educate dog owners about separation anxiety and how they can help minimize this problem in their dogs.

stems from being placed in an unfamiliar situation; by familiarizing him with being alone, he will learn that he will survive. That is not to say you should purposely leave your dog home alone, but the dog needs to know that, while he can depend on you for his care, you do not have to be by his side 24 hours a day.

When the dog is alone in the house, he should be confined to his designated dog-proof area of the house. This should be the area in which he sleeps and already feels comfortable so he will feel more at ease when he is alone.

BARKING

Admittedly, the Pharaoh Hound has more to say than many other dogs, given his superior intelligence and superb way of voicing his concerns. Indeed, barking is a dog's way of "talking." It can be somewhat frustrating because it is not always easy to tell what a dog means by his bark—is he excited, happy, frightened or angry? Whatever it is that the dog is trying to say, he should not be punished for barking. It is only when the barking becomes excessive, and when the excessive barking becomes a bad habit, that the behavior needs to be modified.

Fortunately, Pharaoh Hounds, making excellent alarm dogs, tend to use their barks more

purposefully, though this is not to say entirely discriminately. If an intruder came into your home in the middle of the night and your Pharaoh Hound barked a warning, wouldn't you be pleased? You would probably deem your dog a hero, a wonderful guardian and protector of the home. On the other hand, if a friend drops by unexpectedly and rings the doorbell and is greeted with a sudden sharp bark, you would probably be annoyed at the dog. But in reality, isn't this just the same behavior? The dog does not know any better...unless he sees who is at the door and it is someone he knows, he will bark as a means of vocalizing that his (and your) territory is being threatened. While your friend is not posing a threat, it is all the same to the dog. Barking is his means of letting you know that there is an intrusion, whether friend or foe, on your property. This type of barking is instinctive and should not be discouraged.

Excessive habitual barking, however, is a problem that should be corrected early on. As your Pharaoh Hound grows up, you will be able to tell when his barking is purposeful and when it is for no reason. You will become able to distinguish your dog's different barks and their meanings. For example, the bark when someone comes to the door will be different than the bark

An interesting and harmless device to inhibit excessive barking is worn around the neck. This safe method sprays liquid when activated by the dog's voice box. If your Pharaoh is "barkier" than most, discuss the effectiveness of this device with your vet or a trainer.

when he is excited to see you. It is similar to a person's tone of voice, except that the dog has to rely totally on tone of voice because he does not have the benefit of using words. An incessant barker will be evident at an early age.

There are some things that encourage a dog to bark. For example, if your dog barks non-stop for a few minutes and you give him a treat to quiet him, he believes that you are rewarding him for barking. He will associate barking with getting a treat, and will keep doing it until he is rewarded.

AGGRESSION

Pharaohs are not known to be aggressive, though this is a problem that should concern all responsible dog owners. Aggression can be a problem in dogs of any breed. Aggression, when not controlled, always becomes dangerous. An aggressive dog, no matter the size, may lunge at, bite or even attack a person or another dog. Aggressive behavior is not to be tolerated. It is more than just inappropriate behavior; it is not safe. It is painful for a family to watch their dog become unpredictable in his behavior to the point where they are afraid of him. While not all aggressive behavior is dangerous, things like growling, baring teeth, etc., can be frightening. It is important to ascertain why the dog is acting in this manner. Aggression is a display of dominance, and the dog should not have the dominant role in his pack, which is, in this case, your family.

It is important not to challenge an aggressive dog, as this could provoke an attack. Observe your Pharaoh Hound's body language. Does he make direct eye contact and stare? Does he try to make himself as large as possible: ears pricked, chest out, tail erect? Height and size signify authority in a dog pack—being taller or "above" another dog literally means that he is "above" in social status. These body signals tell you that your Pharaoh Hound thinks he is in charge, a problem that needs to be addressed. An aggressive dog is unpredictable; you never know when he is going to strike and what he is going to do. You cannot understand why a dog

QUIET ON THE SET

To encourage proper barking, you can teach your dog the command "Quiet." When someone comes to the door and the dog barks a few times, praise him. Talk to him soothingly and, when he stops barking, tell him "Quiet" and continue to praise him. In this sense, you are letting him bark his warning, which is an instinctive behavior, and then rewarding him for being quiet after a few barks. You may initially reward him with a treat after he has been quiet for a few minutes.

that is playful one minute is growling the next.

The best solution is to consult a behavioral specialist, one who has experience with the Pharaoh Hound if possible. Together, perhaps you can pinpoint the cause of your dog's aggression and do something about it. An aggressive dog cannot be trusted, and a dog that cannot be trusted is not safe to have as a family pet. If, very unusually, you find that your pet has become untrustworthy and you feel it necessary to seek a new home with a more suitable family and environment, explain fully to the new owners all your reasons for rehoming the dog to be fair to all concerned.

SEXUAL BEHAVIOR

Dogs exhibit certain sexual behaviors that may have influenced your choice of male or female when you first purchased your Pharaoh Hound. To a certain extent, spaying/neutering will eliminate these behaviors, but if you are purchasing a dog that you wish to breed from, you should be aware of what you will have to deal with throughout the dog's life.

Female dogs usually have two estruses per year, with each season lasting about three weeks. These are the only times in which a female dog will mate, and she usually will not allow this until the second week of the cycle, but this does vary from bitch to bitch.

Males tend to mark territory wherever they go, leaving a message for other dogs on trees, poles, fire hydrants, etc.

While most bitches cycle at around six to nine months of age, Pharaoh bitches can have their first season as late as two years of age. If not bred during the heat cycle, it is not uncommon for a bitch to experience a false pregnancy, in which her mammary glands swell and she exhibits maternal tendencies toward toys or other objects.

Behaviors common in unneutered males include wandering, marking territory and mounting. Owners must recognize, though, that mounting is not merely a sexual expression but also one of dominance, seen in males and females alike. Be consistent and persistent and you will find that you can "move mounters."

CHEWING

The national canine pastime is chewing! Every dog loves to sink his "canines" into a tasty bone, but if a bone is not available, most anything will do! Dogs need to chew, to massage their gums, to make their new teeth feel better and to exercise their jaws. This is a natural behavior deeply embedded in all things canine. Our role as owners is not to stop the dog's chewing, but to redirect it to positive, chew-worthy objects. Be an informed owner and purchase proper chew toys like strong nylon bones that will not splinter. Be sure that the objects are safe and durable, since your dog's safety is at risk. Again, the owner is responsible for ensuring a dog-proof environment. The best answer is prevention, that is, put your shoes, handbags and other tasty objects in their proper places (out of the reach of the growing canine

A Pharaoh and his Ibizan Hound friend patrol the property. These alert and protective sighthounds are ready to sound the alarm to warn their owners of anything amiss.

THE MIGHTY MALE

Males, whether castrated or not, will mount almost anything: a pillow, your leg or, much to your dismay, even your neighbor's leg. As with other types of inappropriate behavior, the dog must be corrected while in the act, which for once is not difficult. Often he will not let go! While a puppy is experimenting with his very first urges, his owners feel he needs to "sow his oats" and allow the pup to mount. As the pup grows into a full-size dog, with full-size urges, it becomes a nuisance and an embarrassment. Males always appear as if they are trying to "save the race," more determined and stronger than imaginable. While altering the dog at an appropriate age will limit the dog's desire, it usually does not remove it entirely.

mouth). Direct your puppy to his toy whenever you see him tasting the furniture legs or the leg of your pants. Make a loud noise to attract the pup's attention and immediately escort him to his chew toy. Engage him with the toy for at least four minutes, praising and encouraging him all the while.

Some trainers recommend deterrents, such as hot pepper, a bitter spice or a product designed for this purpose, to discourage the dog from chewing unwanted objects. Test these products with your own dog before investing in large quantities.

A young Pharaoh puppy with a penchant for dirty paws! The tendency to dig varies from dog to dog; when it occurs, it is a behavior you need to discourage or at least control.

JUMPING UP

Jumping up is a dog's friendly way of saying hello! Some dog owners do not mind when their dog jumps up. The problem arises when friends come to the house and the dog greets them in the same manner—whether they like it or not! Pharaohs are selective about their favorite people but the chances are that your visitors will not appreciate your dog's enthusiasm. The dog will not be able to distinguish upon whom he can jump and whom he cannot. Therefore, it is probably best to discourage this behavior entirely.

Pick a command such as "Off" (avoid using "Down" since you will use that for the dog to lie down) and tell him "Off" when he jumps up. Place him on the ground on all fours and have him sit, praising him the whole time.

Always lavish him with praise and petting when he is in the sit position. In this way, you can give him a warm affectionate greeting, let him know that you are as pleased to see him as he is to see you and instill good manners at the same time!

DIGGING

Digging, which is seen as a destructive behavior to humans, is actually quite a natural behavior in dogs. Although terriers (the earth dogs) are most associated with digging, any dog's desire to dig can be irrepressible and most frustrating to his owners. When digging occurs in your yard, it is actually a normal behavior redirected into something the dog can do in his everyday life. In the wild, a dog would be actively seeking food,

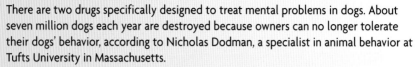

PHARMACEUTICAL FIX

There are two drugs specifically designed to treat mental problems in dogs. About seven million dogs each year are destroyed because owners can no longer tolerate their dogs' behavior, according to Nicholas Dodman, a specialist in animal behavior at Tufts University in Massachusetts.

The first drug, Clomicalm, is prescribed for dogs suffering from separation anxiety, which is said to cause them to react when left alone by barking, chewing their owners' belongings, drooling copiously or defecating or urinating inside the home.

The second drug, Anipryl, is recommended for cognitive dysfunction syndrome or "old-dog syndrome," a mental deterioration that comes with age. Such dogs often seem to forget that they were housebroken and where their food bowls are, and they may even fail to recognize their owners.

A tremendous human-animal bonding relationship is established with all dogs, particularly senior dogs. This precious relationship deteriorates when the dog does not recognize his master. The drug can restore the bond and make senior dogs feel more like their "old selves."

making his own shelter, etc. He would be using his paws in a purposeful manner for his survival. Since you provide him with food and shelter, he has no need to use his paws for these purposes, and so the energy that he would be using may manifest itself in the form of little holes all over your yard and flowerbeds.

Perhaps your dog is digging as a reaction to boredom—it is somewhat similar to someone eating a whole bag of chips in front of the TV—because they are there and there is nothing better to do! Basically, the answer is to provide the dog with adequate play and exercise so that his mind and paws are occupied, and so that he feels as if he is doing something useful.

Of course, digging is easiest to control if it is stopped as soon as possible, but it is often hard to catch a dog in the act. If your dog is a compulsive digger and is not easily distracted by other activities, you can designate an area where he is allowed to dig. If you catch him digging in an off-limits area of the yard, immediately bring him to the approved area and praise him for digging there. Keep a close eye on him so that you can catch him in the act— that is the only way to make him understand what is permitted and what is not. If you take him to a hole he dug an hour ago and tell him "No," he will understand that you are not fond of holes, dirt or flowers. If you catch him while he is stifle-deep in your tulips, that is when he will get your message.

Although behavior problems can be seen in any dog of any breed, the Pharaoh Hound generally makes a stable, dignified pet with whom you'll enjoy sharing your life.

Teething puppies need to soothe their aching gums, which usually means that whatever is in their reach ends up in their mouths (even if it's still attached to your hand!).

FOOD STEALING

Is your dog devising ways of stealing food from your coffee table? If so, you must answer the following questions: Is your Pharaoh Hound hungry, or is he "constantly famished" like many dogs seem to be? Face it, some dogs are more food-motivated than others. They are totally obsessed by the smell of food and can only think of their next meal. Food stealing is terrific fun and always yields a great reward—*food*, glorious food.

The owner's goal, therefore, is to be sensible about where food is placed in the home, and to reprimand your dog whenever he is caught in the act of stealing. But remember, only reprimand your dog if you actually see him stealing, not later when the crime is discovered, for that will be of no use at all and will only serve to confuse him.

BEGGING

Just like food stealing, begging is a favorite pastime of hungry puppies! It achieves that same terrific result—*food!* Dogs quickly learn that their owners keep the "good food" for themselves, and that we humans do not dine on dried food alone. Begging is a conditioned response related to a specific stimulus, time and place. The sounds of the kitchen, cans and bottles opening, crinkling bags, the smell of food in preparation, etc., will excite the dog, and soon the paws are in the air!

Here is the solution to stopping this behavior: *Never give in to a beggar!* You are rewarding the dog for sitting pretty, jumping up, whining and rubbing his nose into you by giving him food. By ignoring the dog, you will (eventually) force the behavior into extinction. Note that the behavior is likely to get worse before it disappears, so be sure there are not any "softies" in the family who will give in to little "Oliver" every time he whimpers, "More, please."

COPROPHAGIA

Feces eating is, to humans, one of the most disgusting behaviors that a dog could engage in, yet to the dog it is perfectly normal. It is hard for us to understand why a dog would want to eat his own feces. He could be seeking certain nutrients that are missing from his diet; he could be just plain hungry; or he could be attracted by the pleasing (to a dog) scent. While coprophagia most often refers to the dog's eating his own feces, a dog may just as likely eat that of another animal as well if he comes across it. Dogs often find the stool of cats and horses more palatable than that of other dogs.

DOGS HAVE FEELINGS, TOO

You probably don't realize how much your dog notices the presence of a new person in your home as well as the loss of a familiar face. If someone new has moved in with you, your pet will need help adjusting. Have the person feed your dog or accompany the two of you on a walk. Also, make sure your roommate is aware of the rules and routines you have already set for your dog.

If you have just lost a longtime companion, there is a chance you could end up with a case of "leave me, leave my dog." Dogs experience separation anxiety and depression, so watch for any changes in sleeping and eating habits and try to lavish a little extra love on your dog. It might make you feel better, too.

Vets have found that diets with a low digestibility, containing relatively low levels of fiber and high levels of starch, increase coprophagia. Therefore, high-fiber diets may decrease the likelihood of dogs' eating feces. Both the consistency of the stool (how firm it feels in the dog's mouth) and the presence of undigested nutrients increase the likelihood. Once the dog develops diarrhea from feces eating, he will likely stop this distasteful habit.

To discourage this behavior, first make sure that the food you are feeding your dog is nutritionally complete and that he is getting enough food. If changes in his diet do not seem to work, and no medical cause can be found, you will have to modify the behavior through environmental control before it becomes a habit. The best way to prevent your dog from eating his stool is to make it unavailable—clean up after he eliminates and remove any stool from the yard. If it is not there, he cannot eat it.

Reprimanding for stool eating rarely impresses the dog. Vets recommend distracting the dog while he is in the act of stool eating. Coprophagia is seen most frequently in pups 6 to 12 months of age, and usually disappears around the dog's first birthday.

INDEX

Page numbers in **boldface** indicate illustrations.

My Pharaoh Hound

PUT YOUR PUPPY'S FIRST PICTURE HERE

Dog's Name _____

Date _____ Photographer _____